BCK —

a little reference
material for your
next project

CVC
August 30, 1991

Treehouses

Lady Amelia Paget's treehouse at Plas Newydd, Anglesey

Treehouses

ANTHONY AIKMAN

ROBERT HALE · LONDON

© Anthony Aikman 1988
First published in Great Britain 1988

Robert Hale Limited
Clerkenwell House
Clerkenwell Green
London EC1R 0HT

British Library Cataloguing in Publication Data
Aikman, Anthony
Treehouses.
1. Tree houses
I. Title
728'.9   NA8470
ISBN 0-7090-3152-1

Design by Joanna Restall

Set in Linotron 202 Sabon by
Rowland Phototypesetting Limited
Bury St Edmunds, Suffolk
Printed in Great Britain by
St Edmundsbury Press Limited, Bury St Edmunds,
Suffolk and bound by WBC Bookbinders Limited

Contents

	List of Illustrations	7
	Acknowledgements	11
	Preface	15
	Introduction	17
1	In the Beginning	25
2	Treehouses of Europe	33
3	Stately Treehouses, Old and New	49
4	In Search of Treehouses	73
5	Hollow Trees	92
6	Treehouse Adaptations	109
7	Treehouses Around the World	135
8	Fantasy Treehouses	155
9	Build Your Own Treehouse	167
	Index	189

In memory of my grandfather, the late H. F. MacMillan FLS, Curator of the Royal Botanical Garden, Peradeniya, Ceylon, 1895–1925

Illustrations

Lady Amelia Paget's treehouse at Plas Newydd, Anglesey	*Frontispiece*
The House in the Tree pub at Haydens Elm, near Gloucester	14
Clifford Matthews' hollow elm house	16
Pitchford Hall treehouse from the north	19
The author's first treehouse in the Solomon Islands	21
The author's treehouse in St Margaret's Bay	22
Print of a Japanese treewalk from Kyoto	24
Nest-dwellers on a South Sea island	26
Tree-dwellers on the Orinoco river, Venezuela	27
Airy dwellings in the Orinoco Delta	28
A Persian seat in the branches of a tree	29
The Bradford Table Carpet	30–1
An Italian 'hermitage' in a garden	34
A bower made by interlacing trees	35
The Medicean treehouse at Pratolino, near Florence	36
Brueghel's *Lechery*	38–9
Painting of a treehouse by Hans Bol	40
The Treeman – a detail from Hieronymus Bosch's *The Garden of Earthly Delights*	43
The treehouse at Cobham Hall	44
John Evelyn's treehouse at Wotton in Surrey	45
A Victorian treehouse bower	46
The treehouse looking towards Pitchford Hall	48
An Ordnance Survey map showing Pitchford Hall	51
An interior view of Pitchford treehouse	54
An eighteenth-century view of Pitchford treehouse	59

Treehouses and treewalks at Belton House Adventure Park	63
Fort Alamo at Belton Park	64
The treehouse at Heale House	67
'Cuckoo!'	69
The Downings' treehouse from below	72
A section of the Downings' suspension bridge	75
The Downings' treehouse	76
Village postcard showing Rolleston treehouse	79
Ralph Curry's treehouse near Canterbury	81
Ralph Curry's mini treehouse	83
The lower floor of the treehouse in Chilham Woods	85
The stairway and terrace, Chilham Woods	86
Fort Road treehouse, Gosport	88
The smallest treehouse in the world	90
Hollow treehouses at the Happy Eater of Hogs Back, Surrey	93
Robin Hood's hollow oak in Sherwood Forest	98
The famous Cowthorpe Oak	99
The Rosemaund Oak in 1870	100
Church bell in a yew tree at Barfreston, near Canterbury	102
The lighthouse of the Tally Ho pub near Wokingham	105
Le Chêne Classé	108
Print of a Chinese treehouse	110
Treehouse restaurants at Plessis Robinson	112
General view of Le Chêne Classé	115
A Chinese tree	116
The chapel of Notre Dame in the hollow oak at Allouville	119
An early photograph of the Old House in the Tree	120
German POWs delivering barrels to the House in the Tree pub	123
The treehouse in St John's Wood churchyard	124
Tree walk, Battersea Fun Fair, 1951	126
An unusual station at Moreton-on-Lugg	128
'Eve' at Moreton station, 1870	129
The Tree with a Road in It	131
The old oak, Worlingham	133
Treetops, 1932	134
Treetops, 1952	137
Treetops today	138
A treehouse in New Guinea	141

Sketch of a lean-to platform	143
A hide for culling deer	144
A treehouse in the Californian Redwood forests	146
A handmade house in California	147
The highest treehouse in the world	152
John Morland's treehouse tree	154
John Morland's hospital tree	157
Up in the Milly-Molly-Mandy nest	160
Christopher Robin's treehouse	162
On the top of the Crumpetty Tree	163
A sketch from *The Wizard King*	165
Pooh Bear visiting Owl's old world residence	168
Ralph Curry's residence among the treetops near Canterbury	170
The Downings' moated treehouse under construction	172
Angled supports and frame	174
Slots and bolts and nailed crossmembers	175
The platform	175
Hut frame and thatching	177
Roof construction	178
Ladders	180
Water filter	184
Map: Treehouses of Britain	12–13

Acknowledgements

Chris Cromarty (sketches): 12–13; British Museum: 38–9, 40; Bridgeman Art Library/Prado, Madrid: 43; Ordnance Survey, Crown Copyright Reserved: 12–13, 51; The Photo Source: 137; John Morland: 154, 157; Joyce Lankester Brisley/Harrap: 160; Copyright E. H. Shepard under the Berne Convention, reproduced by permission of Curtis Brown Ltd., London: 162, 168; all other sketches by the author.

Acknowledgements

My sincere thanks to all those who made this book possible, including:
David Aikman; Peter Aikman; Amanda Arrowsmith; Anthony Bayliss, Normandy; Commander Bellars, Cobham Hall; Jay Boyce; Jean Broom, Chartwell; Anthea Brown, Bodenham Hall; Mr Brown; Leonard Cogswell; Caroline Colthurst, Pitchford Hall; Ralph Curry; John and Leslie Downing, Chediston; John Forgie, National Trust; C. A. Green, Shrewsbury; A. Haney; Sarah Holloway; Rev. Geoffrey Johnson; John Lawrence, House in the Tree pub; P. J. Loobey; John McVery; John Martell; Clifford Matthews, Ventnor; Sir Yehudi Menuhin; John and Jan Morland; Brian Nice, Tally Ho pub; Susan Owens, Rhos-on-Sea; S. P. W. J. Simpson, River Dart Country Park; Bettina Stapleton, Wookey Hole; Marion Stewart, Churchill College; Mrs Anthea Tonkin, Woolhope Naturalists Club; A. Youel; *et al.*

Special thanks to Paula Henderson for her advice and guidance and to Connie Jewell for her help and encouragement throughout the preparation of the book.

I am grateful for permission to reproduce copyright material from the following books:

James K. Baxter, poem *The Tree House* (Price Milburn)
Enid Blyton, *The Magic Faraway Tree* (Deans)
Arthur Bryant, *King Charles II* (Longman)
Sarah Churchill, *A Thread in the Tapestry* (Deutsch)
John Hillaby, *Journey through England* (Constable)
A. A. Milne, *Winnie-the-Pooh* (Methuen Children's Books)
R. P. Straughan, *Build a Jungle Zoo*
Joanna Stubbs, *The Tree House* (Deutsch)
Eric Sherbrooke Walker, *Treetops Hotel* (Robert Hale)

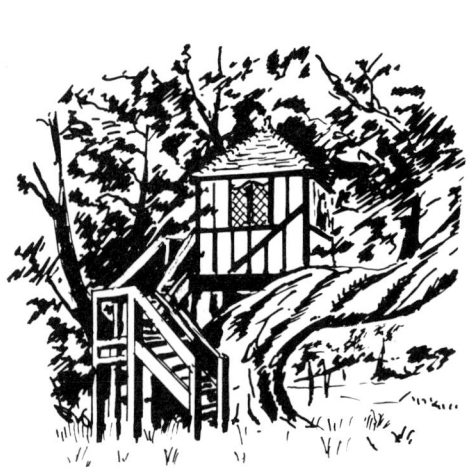

Pitchford Hall treehouse

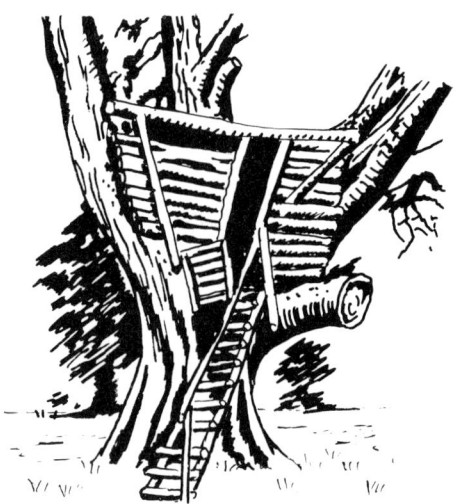

Lady Amelia Paget's treehouse

Miles
0
100
0
km
150

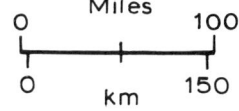

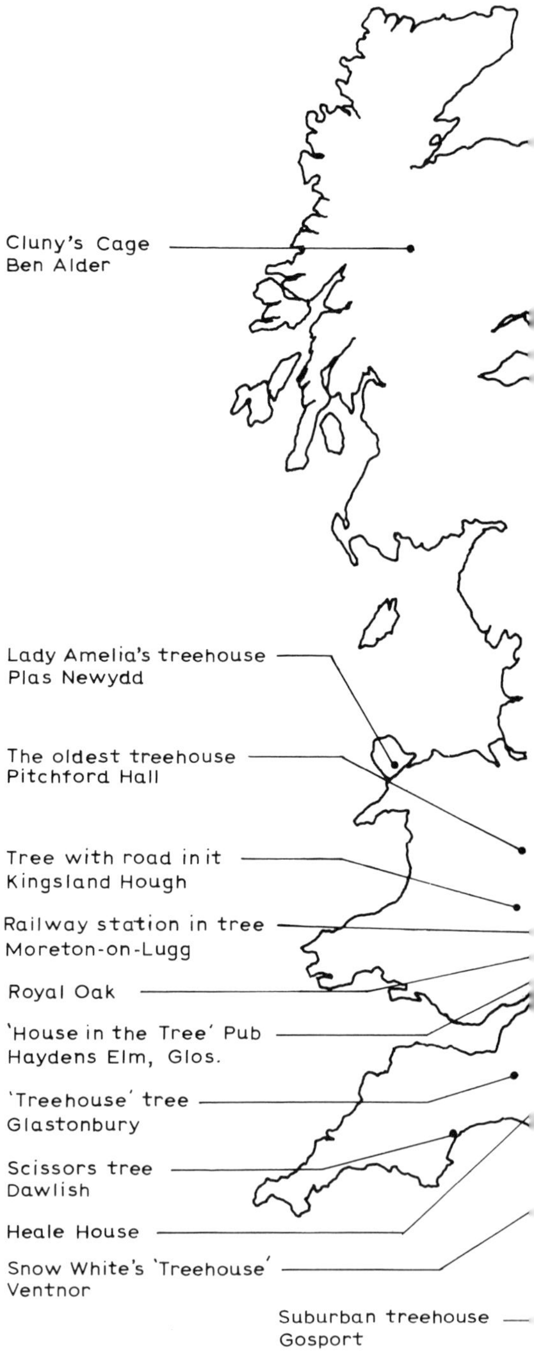

Cluny's Cage
Ben Alder
Lady Amelia's treehouse
Plas Newydd
The oldest treehouse
Pitchford Hall
Tree with road in it
Kingsland Hough
Railway station in tree
Moreton-on-Lugg
Royal Oak
'House in the Tree' Pub
Haydens Elm, Glos.
'Treehouse' tree
Glastonbury
Scissors tree
Dawlish
Heale House
Snow White's 'Treehouse'
Ventnor
Suburban treehouse
Gosport

Treehou

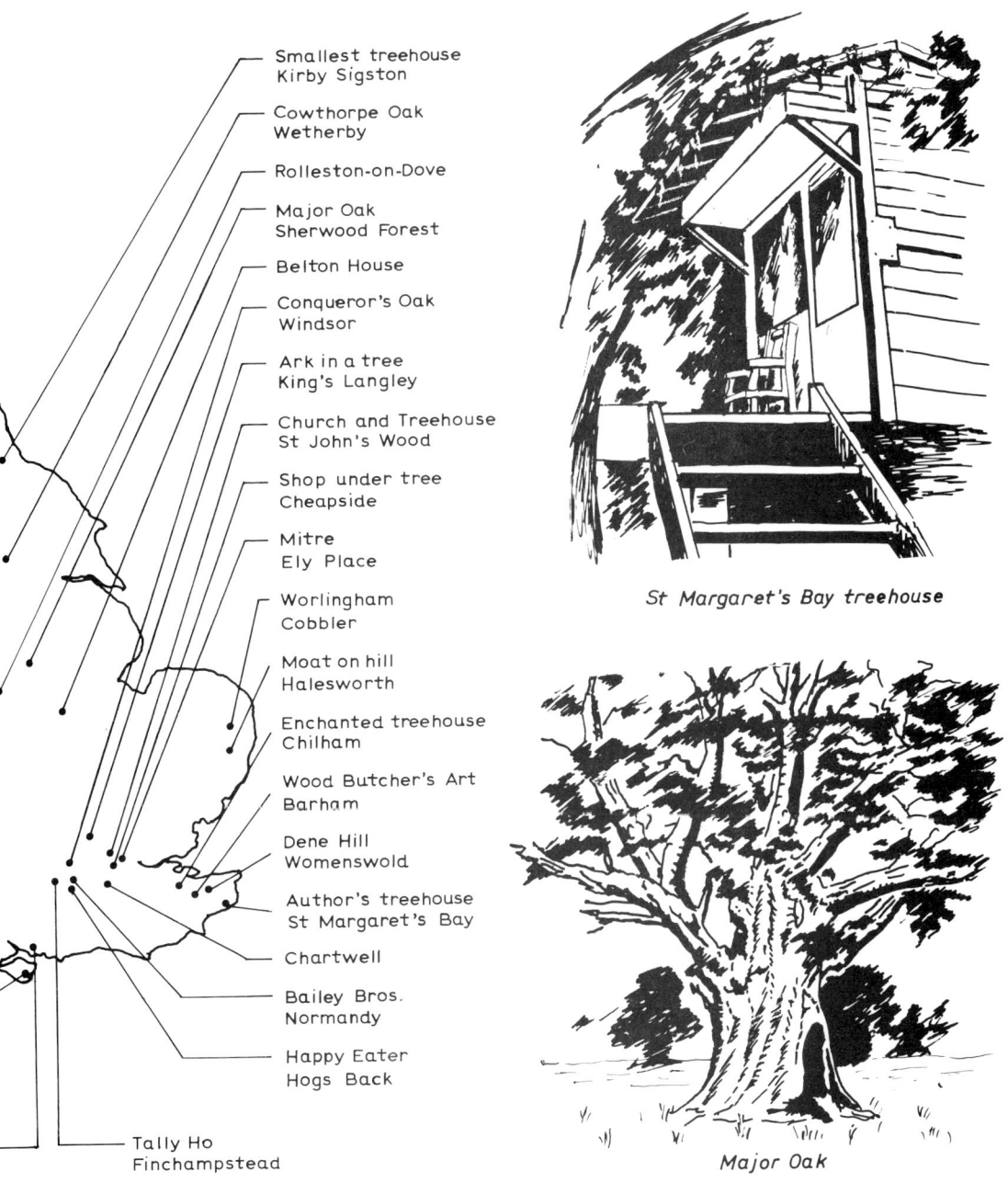

The inn sign of The House in the Tree pub at Haydens Elm, near Gloucester. Cider was served from barrels in the treehouse

Preface

Queen Elizabeth I banqueted in a treehouse in Kent, Elizabeth II was proclaimed Queen in one in Kenya, Victoria spent a sketching holiday in one which still exists near Shrewsbury. The Emperor Caligula feasted in them, castaways have lived in them, authors from A. A. Milne to Major Charles Gibson have written about them, Bosch and Brueghel painted frightening allegorical scenes in them, Robin Hood and his outlaws sheltered in them, hunters use them as hides. Treehouses have been adapted to the most extraordinary purposes: there are pubs in trees, churches in trees and even a railway station in a tree.

The hollow elm that Clifford Matthews converted into a pleasant two-storey residence at his home near Ventnor on the Isle of Wight

Introduction

Treehouses have always held a special appeal in our imaginations. For many of us they belong to the adventurous days of childhood. Later, when our own children try to build them in the back garden with a packing case, some rusty nails and a scrap of old linoleum, we relive those 'balmier' days, when a few boards lashed to petrol cans became the *Hispaniola*, and a treehouse one's very own Robinson Crusoe island. Practical too, for an illicit cigarette, escaping from doing the washing-up or being nagged to get on with one's homework.

As soon as we learn to read, we discover treehouses. Winnie-the-Pooh's friend Owl lived in one, and Pooh Bear was always on the move from one tree residence to another in his insatiable search for honey. Old Tarzan films are still shown on television, featuring magnificent treehouses complete with all sorts of enviable attractions – hammocks, rope ladders, coconuts to drink from, bananas within easy reach for breakfast, and all the animals of the jungle tame and friendly. 'The Swiss Family Robinson' were so content with treehouse life on their castaway island that they refused to leave when a ship finally came to their rescue.

Most of us can remember playing at Robin Hood and looking for a suitable hollow tree for a base camp. At school we learned how King Charles II hid in the boughs of a tree at Boscobel after the Battle of Worcester while the Roundheads were busy searching for him on the ground below.

Treehouses offer an escape route into a fantasy world, and although most of us would never consider building one, many might imagine doing so. In a letter to me the famous violinist

Sir Yehudi Menuhin writes: 'I infinitely prefer the idea of a treehouse to that of living in a cave! Yet, I suppose a cosy cave could correspond to a version of a town house, whereas the treehouse would be my country residence. I can imagine a treehouse being the ultimate in sheer enjoyment – close to rustling leaves, soft breezes, the scent of blossoms, birdsong, built on a stout branch and comfortably feathered like a nest . . .'

During many and varied travels in some of the remote parts of the world, I have lived in caves and treehouses and can positively recommend the latter. Every cave I occupied was invariably damp and smelly. It filled with smoke the moment I lit a fire, and often had its own permanent resident of smaller or greater size, who quite naturally became indignant on finding an intruder. I was once drying out my clothes in a cave on the slopes of Mount Elgon in East Africa when an elephant came charging out! Treehouses are infinitely safer and more versatile! Italians use them as 'hides' for hunting; Indian fakirs spend months, even years, meditating up in them; Meru tribesmen in Kenya live in them to guard their cattle and goats from wild beasts. There are tribes in Papua, New Guinea, who build treehouses in which to place their dead; these dwellings are then revered as the homes of their ancestors. In Southern Africa, farmers of all races carve out the insides of the large, succulent Baobab trees to use as cooling and storage chambers. And some perfectly sane people build treehouses to live or entertain in.

Perhaps the world's most famous treehouse was 'Treetops' in Kenya, where Princess Elizabeth was staying when George VI died, and where she took the oath of accession to the throne. But treehouses are not new to royalty. Regal banquets have been held in them from the days of Emperor Caligula to those of Queen Elizabeth I. At the other end of the social scale – according to the Wiltshire Quarter sessions of 1647, some people without a roof over their heads, 'Were constrained to dwelle in hollowe trees . . .' On Worlingham Common, Suffolk in 1785, the local cobbler set up shop in one. The Beatles singer John Lennon built a treehouse in his Liverpool back garden overlooking the Strawberry Fields orphanage about which he later wrote a song. A hollow tree became for a while a ticket office on the Great Western Railway; there is a pub in the West Country where 'cider was served from barrels in a

Pitchford Hall treehouse from the north. No wonder young Princess Victoria was enchanted with it

tree', and to this very day there is a church in a tree in Normandy.

My original attraction to treehouses was inspired by my grandfather, the botanist and explorer H. F. MacMillan, for many years curator of the Royal Botanical Gardens at Peradeniya in Ceylon (now Sri Lanka) and author of *Tropical Planting and Gardening*. At Peradeniya he collected seeds and plants from all over the world, including the giant Amazon Lily – *Victoria Regia*, whose leaves are so large they will take the weight of a man.

I grew up believing that botany was in my blood, and when I left school I chose to study forestry at Bangor University. I had the romantic illusion that a forestry career would mean a cottage in the country, a sheepdog, a shotgun, a wife in wellies and a couple of carefree children. Life has an unfortunate habit of not turning out in the way one expects, and even though I left university with a degree in forestry, I still couldn't tell one tree from another. My first job was with the Kent County Council. I hastily purchased *The Observer's Book of*

Trees but unfortunately it was autumn and the leaves were falling!

My first experience of treehouses came when I went to the Solomon Islands. I was helping at a mission station on the north coast of Guadalcanal. It was very isolated. To get to town there were a dozen rivers to ford, and in the rainy season these were often impassable. The mission was virtually self-sufficient. The children who went to school there had their own gardens in forest clearings along the river bank, where they grew yams, cassava and Chinese cabbage, and built their communal huts. Island huts were roomy affairs on stilts, with thatched roofs and walls. Following their example, I decided to build my own, with a couple of helpers and a rusty machete. The machete is the island multi-purpose tool. It digs holes, chops wood, clears brush, scrapes copra out of coconuts and builds huts. My hut was built without a single nail. The whole frame fitted together in chopped-out notches; long, overlapping palm fronds were bound together to thatch the roof and walls. The floor was covered with split canes and a huge mat woven from coconut fibre. Unfortunately I built the hut too close to the river, and it was washed away during the first storm.

I spent that night up a tree, but it gave me an idea, and when I built my second hut it was firmly secured among the selfsame branches, out of reach of floods and with a fine view from its verandah, up river towards Papamanchua – the central peak on the island.

Papamanchua was a South Seas Mount Olympus. Here the equivalent of Zeus and Hera and the rest of the gods reigned. At night, when thunder and lightning played on the volcanic peak – as they frequently did, the islanders shook their heads in awe. The gods were arguing again!

The next time I stayed in a treehouse was in the Philippines. There are literally thousands of islands dotting the South China Seas, but few can be more beautiful than Boracay, a white-sand, coral atoll just off the northern tip of Panay – an island paradise reached by outrigger canoe where the only accommodation is among the scattering of thatched huts under the waving coconut palms. One of the more enterprising islanders had built a number of treehouse residences in some giant mangoes. They were beautifully constructed affairs with verandahs on all sides and reached by a ladder up

The author's first treehouse in the Solomon Islands, looking up river towards Mount Papamanchua, fabled home of the gods

The author's treehouse in St Margaret's Bay. Supported by the branches of a giant sycamore which stands halfway up the cliffs

to a trapdoor in the floor. There is no electricity on Boracay, nor are there any roads. Footpaths connect the tiny villages, and at night lanterns made from Coca-cola cans flicker like fireflies among the trees.

It is often no simple matter to account for things one does, and I have no easy explanation why I built myself a treehouse at St Margaret's Bay, in Kent. It was not the first by any means. Our local doctor built a fine one high up the pine trees in the grounds of his house overlooking the bay. What always intrigued me was that the bottom step of the ladder pinned to the tree trunk was a hospital crutch!

My own treehouse is supported by a giant sycamore, half way up the cliffs. In front there is a rather rickety verandah with ladders leading down to *terra firma*. At the rear a plank used to be the sole means of access. At one stage, after the hut was burgled, I developed a fortress complex and replaced the plank with a drawbridge and a row of sharpened stakes below. The narrow escape of the vicar who was making a social call one evening put an end to this.

'My dear boy,' he exclaimed breathlessly as he clung to the branches, 'for a moment I felt my ultimate demise was upon me!'

As a result, my uncle and aunt on whose land – or air – the treehouse rests, ordered me to remove the fortifications or make myself personally responsible for any claims for damages.

I shall be discussing later various ways one can build treehouses. Suffice to say mine is box-shaped with a sloping roof thatched in straw, and a sleeping attic under it. A twelve-volt battery – supplemented by candles – powers the lighting. A hand pump supplies the sink, from which a flexible drainaway tube leads out below. An old cast-iron stove from a British Rail guard's van provides heat. The walls are lined with felt to keep the draughts out, and various layers of carpets cover the floor. The loo used to be a funnel outside, protected by an umbrella, but nowadays a minute annexe contains a 'Porta Potti' chemical toilet, making the whole place a lot more civilized. A sofa, a writing-desk and a few cane chairs comprise the furniture. A spare bed in the shape of a hammock from Guatemala is stored hooked to the ceiling. There's not room to stretch this inside. It has to hang suspended between neighbouring branches. After loading a guest on board, one simply lets go and hammock and occupant sail away into mid air for the night. Once I overslept and discovered a rather woebegone figure desperately paddling the air in a vain attempt to reach the verandah.

A permanent guest is an overfed squirrel which takes its meals on the verandah and pops about the branches. It has the unendearing habit of divebombing the roof. Several pounds of solid squirrel landing repeatedly inches above one's head at the crack of dawn is not the best way to begin the day.

For all its drawbacks – and there are many – the treehouse has a spectacular view. Through the tips of the waving pines one looks across the Dover Straits to the white cliffs of France. At night the waves breaking on the beach far below lull one to sleep.

Print of a Japanese treewalk from Kyoto. Set high among the leafy branches, such treewalks were popular venues for admiring nature

In the Beginning

The Nesting Instinct

In the beginning, the ancestors of man and apes lived in trees. Since then many, but not all, of both species have come down to earth. Certain chimpanzees make simple nests in the branches, day nests and night nests, and just as fashion-conscious ladies would never dream of being seen in the same dress twice, these apes never return to the same nest. Their day nests are reserved solely for siestas as most apes, like many humans, enjoy a two-hour nap between 9.30 a.m. and 3 p.m.

One of the most elaborate nests of the ape family is built by the nocturnal lemur. It cuts up twigs and carries them aloft, where it weaves them into a globe-like nest high in the treetops. The nests are completely roofed over and have a small side entrance and a floor lined with shredded leaves. There is generally room for one adult.

Li Chi, the ancient book of Chinese ritual, claims that in remotest antiquity, 'The people had no houses. In winter they lived in caves which they had excavated and in summer they lived in nests in the trees, which they built on frames.'

When Captain Cook discovered Australia, he found to his surprise that the Aborigines in Tasmania (now extinct) lived in treetops 'like fauns and satyrs'. This habit was widespread among certain South Sea islands. The nests were thatched with crude shelters, and the inhabitants lowered themselves to the ground in large baskets woven from supple shoots and coconut matting. This is depicted in the drawing from *Tien-shih chai hua-pao* on p. 26.

The tree-dwelling habit was not confined to the southern

Nest-dwellers on a South Sea island, an old engraving from Tien-shih chai hua-pao. Note the use of baskets to get up and down – perhaps tree-dwellers were the inventors of the first lift?

oceans. The Roman historian Tacitus records in his *Germania* that the Fenni (today's Lapps) ' ... lived in astonishing barbarism and disgusting misery. They had no fixed houses, nor had their infants any shelter against wild beasts and rain except the covering given by a few intertwined branches.'

After Christopher Columbus opened the way for exploration of the Americas, there were various reportings of human tree-dwellers. Sir Walter Raleigh in *The Discovery of the Empire of Guiana* relates how a tribe along the Orinoco delta, called the Tiñitiñas, were 'A very goodlie people. Dwell upon the trees where they build very artificiall townes and villages.'

There was a good and practical reason for this. Quite apart from offering protection from raiding tribes, it enabled them to escape the worst of the swarms of mosquitoes that emerge from the forest at nightfall. Mosquitoes cannot fly far over water.

Sir Walter Raleigh was not the only one to discover people living in trees in that region. Engravings in Erasmus Francisci's *Lustgarten* (1668) identify Spanish invaders attacking the natives, besieged in their tree 'nests'. As the print shows, so long as their ammunition of rocks and coconuts, spears and arrows lasted, the tree-dwellers were in an advantageous position. Unfortunately for them, the Spanish conquistadors protecting themselves with boards from the rocks raining on them, got to work with axes. Having felled the trees and tree nests, they put the tree-dwellers – including women with babes in arms – ruthlessly to the sword. Other tree nests were bombarded with flights of spears – however, the cunning tree-dwellers are shown catching some of these and hurling them back.

To this day there are tribes living along the periodically flooded riverlands in the Amazonian rainforests who escape floods and bugs by building simple platforms among the trees. In the river deltas of Venezuela they often use the Itá palm trunks as supporting posts for the platforms, a lower one to cook on, an upper serving as a roof. Hammocks for sleeping are strung between the trees.

One of the earliest pictorial examples of treehouses surviving in England is shown on the Bradford Table Carpet – a tapestry screen made for the Earl of Bradford between 1605 and 1615. It was designed to depict stages in man's relationship to nature. As Sir Walter Raleigh's *The Discovery of the Empire of Guiana* was first published in 1596, it is quite likely that this had some influence on the tapestry.

Tree-dwellers on the Orinoco river, Venezuela. From Hulsius's Fünffte kurtze wunderbare Beschreibung

A nineteenth-century engraving showing the airy dwellings in the Orinoco Delta where the Itá palm forms solid posts for platforms and roofs

Treehouses of the Roman Empire

In England, as we shall see later, tree bowers first became widely popular in Tudor times, but the earliest historical evidence of treehouses as venues of entertainment comes from the Roman Pliny the Elder, writing in his *Natural History*, 1,500 years earlier. He records that in the Roman province of Lycia there was a huge hollow plane tree beside the road, close to a cool spring. The space inside was so big that Licinius Mucianus, who was consul for the province, 'once held a banquet in it with eighteen members of his retinue'. According to Pliny, 'He enjoyed himself more among the foliage than amid the splendours of marble halls.'

Plane trees (*Platinus*) grow to immense size in Greece and southern Italy, where they shade many a village square. Pliny also mentions that the Emperor Caligula had on his estates a plane tree of such breadth and size that benches were arranged on the branches and a banquet was held up in the tree, in a 'dining-room' large enough for fifteen guests plus their servants. It was pleasantly shady, and Pliny cattily adds that

A Persian painting of a seat in the branches of a tree

The Bradford Table Carpet made for the Earl of Bradford 1605–15

much of the shade was cast by Caligula himself, who was fat enough to block out the sun.

In those days the main meal would have been taken in mid-afternoon. One can picture Caligula's guests reclining on couches up in the tree attended by servants who replenished their silver drinking bowls with honeyed wine, and even washed their hands between courses. Roman feasts are well recorded. Extracts from a menu by Apicius include such appetizers (*gusti*) as sow's udder stuffed with salted sea urchins, followed by the main course, which hosts went to great lengths to make as exotic as possible and which might include boiled ostrich with sweet sauce, turtle dove boiled in its feathers, roast parrot, dormice stuffed with pork and pine kernels, flamingo boiled with dates. No wonder Romans frequently were sick during the meals! Accompanying all this gormandizing, Caligula's treehouse echoed to the sweet music of strummed lyres while the guests were beguiled by professional entertainers – jugglers, acrobats and Nubian dancing girls.

Oriental Treehouses

In Persia treehouses were very popular from the seventeenth century. Old paintings show platforms set up in trees with stairways leading to them. Some of these 'houses' were most elaborate – richly decorated with gold and silver. They even had running water and fountains playing! Up here, in their leafy platforms, catching the most of any breeze, the Persian nobility enjoyed themselves, feasting and relaxing.

In India, where the tree was frequently symbolized as the pillar of the universe, the Mogul emperors sometimes sat in tree thrones, set amongst the lower branches, while their ministers attended below. Hindu monks and hermits frequently lived in hermitages up among the boughs of the 'sacred' Oriental plane tree, their minds freed from earthbound considerations.

The Japanese constructed platforms and walkways on tall bamboo scaffolding that raised them up into the branches. From time immemorial they built these structures in their gardens but rarely used them for entertaining. They were chiefly regarded as viewing platforms, a means of enjoying the garden and the foliage from a 'bird's-eye' view.

Treehouses of Europe

During the Middle Ages the monasteries first popularized treehouses in Europe. The monks built themselves little hermitages up in the trees. As this fourteenth-century miniature shows, they were simple rooms open to the front, with the benefits of shade and breeze in which the monks could work at their manuscripts and meditate.

The Italian Renaissance

It was in Italy that treehouses reached their peak of popularity and design. The rebirth of art and culture which spread throughout Europe in the late Middle Ages embraced landscape gardening along with all the other arts and sciences. Here some of the most beautiful treehouses ever built were created for the Medici dukes at their villas outside Florence – notably at Castello and Pratolino.

From humble peasant origins the Medici family had risen to become merchant princes and rulers of Florence. At the same time they were powerful patrons of the arts. The treehouse at Villa Castello was built during the time of Cosimo I, a great-nephew of Lorenzo de' Medici, '*Il Magnifico*'. As well as being a financial genius and bringing great wealth to Florence, Cosimo encouraged both the arts and sciences, and shortly after his rise to power he commissioned the architect Tribolo to build Villa Castello, on the lower slopes of Monte Merello, a particularly lovely site. The plains sloped away to the River Arno, and in front of the villa were two large lakes filled from an ancient Roman aqueduct.

Once the house was built, Tribolo set about landscaping the

An Italian miniature, c. 1400, showing a monastic 'hermitage' in a garden. A safe retreat for contemplation or for sorting out the monastery accounts

garden. There were terraces and avenues and orchards, and in a meadow to the east of the villa he planted a holm oak '... so thickly covered with ivy that it looked like a thicket.' He constructed a stepped walkway climbing up into it, and at the top a large platform and seats '... with backs all of living green. And in the middle a marble table with a vase of variegated marble into which water is brought by a pipe, which spouts into the air and is carried off by another pipe.' The description is by Vasari, who visited Castello often. He adds: 'The pipes are so covered with ivy that they cannot be seen and the water is controlled by taps. It is impossible to describe how the water is carried along the branches of this tree, to sprinkle people and to make fearful hissing sounds...'

It is quite likely that Tribolo got his idea from reading *Hypnerotomachia Poliphili* written by a Dominican monk, Francesco Colonna. In this poetic story of a journey through an imaginary landscape, the narrator finds himself in an arbour formed by the intertwined branches of fruit trees: 'The bowghes were so artificially twisted and growne together that

A bower made by interlacing trees. From an agricultural treatise by Piero de Crescenzi which shows the painted ceiling of Sala dello Asse, Castello Sforzesco, Milan

you might ascend up by them and not bee scene in them, nor yet the way where you went up.'

The art of interlacing branches into bowers is described in an agricultural treatise by Piero de Crescenzi and an illustration is seen on the painted ceiling of the Sala delle Asse, Castello Sforzesco, in Milan.

Cosimo I was succeeded by his son Francesco, a suspicious despot who raised taxes and all but crippled Tuscany's econ-

The Medicean treehouse at Pratolino, near Florence. Jetting fountains, a spiralling stairway and marble decorations made this one of the most outstanding treehouses ever

omy. One of his few good points was his patronage of the arts, in which he almost exceeded his father. Not content with Castello, he had his own villa built, Villa Pratolino, and here too he had a treehouse constructed. It was called 'La Fonte delle Rovere' – 'The Fountain of the Oak'.

To outdo the treehouse at Castello, Francesco encircled the holm oak at Pratolino with not one but two staircases! They spiralled up, parallel to one another on opposite sides of the tree. Stepped ramps rather than staircases, they led high up to where a platform eight metres in diameter had been created among the topmost branches. On this platform were a marble table, seats and fountains that were fed from water piped along the branches.

Fortunately there are still in existence prints of this treehouse, notably a seventeenth-century engraving by Stephano della Bella.

Fynnes Morrison, one of those intrepid English travellers who wandered around Europe keeping a journal of everything he saw, visited Castello and Pratolino in 1594. Michel de Montaigne, the famous French writer, philosopher and essayist, mentions them during his travels to Italy, Switzerland and Bavaria in 1580.

But tastes in landscape gardening changed. Terraces and strictly formal patterns became popular. The romanticism of the previous century was considered barbaric. The treehouses fell into disrepair and eventually collapsed. Old age, lightning or the axe put an end to the great oak trees in which they had been built. At Villa Petrai outside Florence, however, a similar rustic stairway encircling the great oak survived into the present century, long after the platform it was built for had gone. The holm oak flourishes to this day.

Switzerland, Germany and the Netherlands

During the sixteenth and seventeenth centuries the fashion for treehouses became widespread throughout Europe. As Fynnes Morrison continued his journeys north, he found similar treehouses across the Alps in Switzerland. The only difference was that they were adapted for the cooler climate and the more practical nature of the people. He describes a treehouse at Schaffhausen, complete with windows and doors, and with taps 'which could at a turn divert water into vessels, or for washing glasses'. For the Swiss watchmaking mentality, water

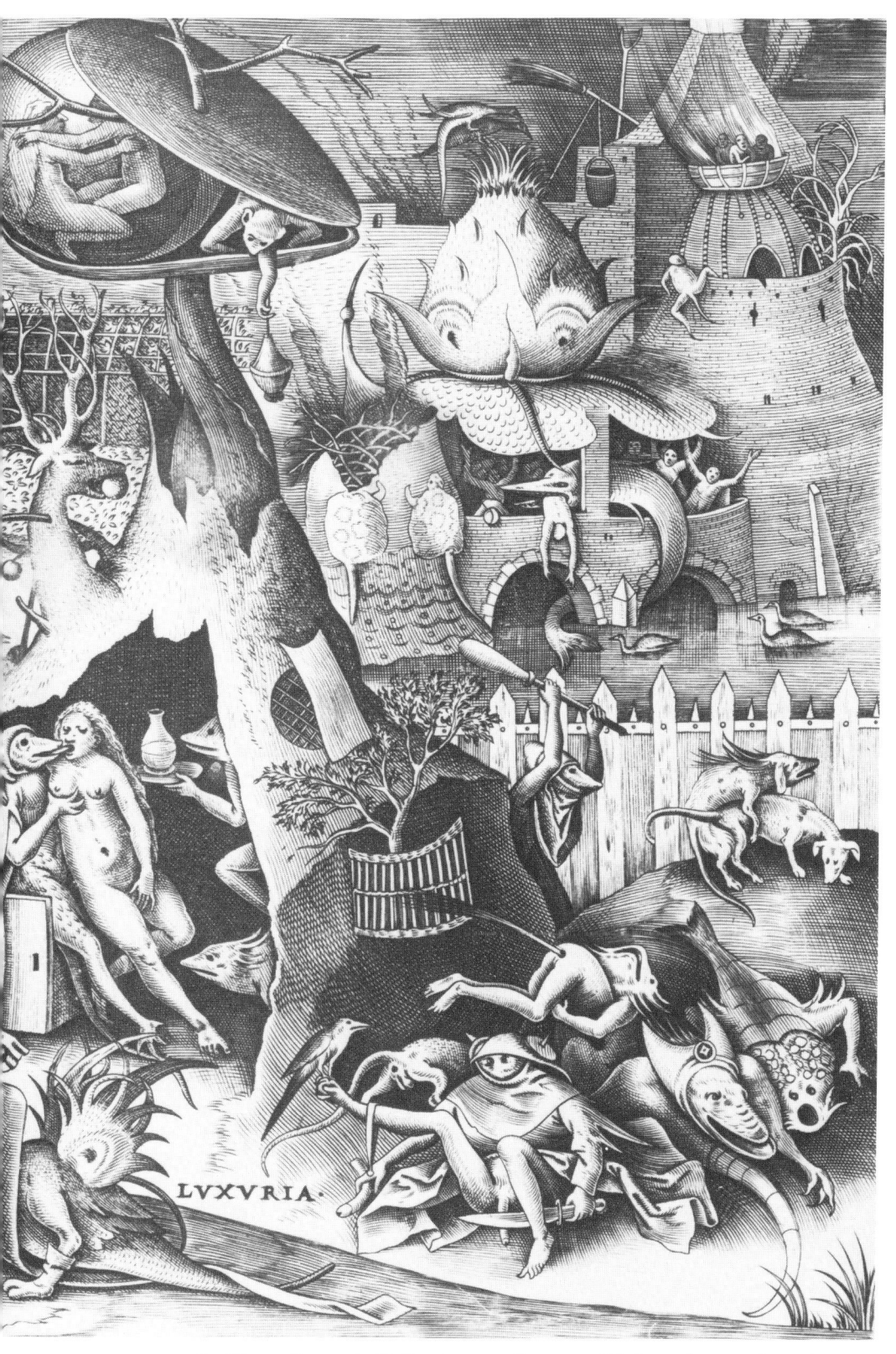

In Pieter Brueghel's Lechery, *all sorts of debauchery takes place in, under and up trees and treehouses*

Painting of a treehouse by Hans Bol. The treehouse is connected to the main building by a bridge and is typical of Dutch treehouses of the period

had work to do, not just to be wasted in fountains as in frivolous Italy.

Travelling further north, the Englishman reported that in the castle grounds at Hainhausen the kitchen courtyard had fountains that were flanked by two tall lime trees into which rooms and seats had been built in different tiers.

In the Netherlands treehouses had been popular since the Renaissance, mainly as arbours supported by a tall, thin tree in the centre. Hans Vriedenen de Vries describes Flemish treehouses in his *Hortorium Viridariorumque* of 1585, and examples of these can be seen in some of the paintings of Hans Bol. A particularly pretty example is that showing a treehouse completely enclosed by interlacing branches with small windows and a door. A charming addition is a bridge linking the treehouse to the main house.

Pieter Brueghel also painted treehouses and tree arbours in some of his remarkable landscapes. A fine example of a two-storey tree arbour is depicted in *Spring*. Published by Hieronymus Cock in 1570, the painting shows men busily preparing the garden and weaving vines onto an elaborate pergola. In the distance couples are dancing on the upper level of an arboured treehouse. Below them, in the shelter of the leafy canopy, other guests are feasting and courting, entertained by a cellist.

In Brueghel's series of moralistic, allegorical paintings, all sorts and designs of treehouses are depicted. In *Anger* a human victim is being turned on a spit over a fire in the base of a hollow tree. While the Devil is basting the victim with a ladle, higher up the tree a tent protects a bell that a monk is tolling. On other branches hang utensils and a large fish. In *Patience*, typical Brueghelesque figures perform all sorts of acts of debauchery around a hollow tree in whose branches a platform, protected by a canopy supports a barrel of wine being readily tapped, a musician playing the lute and a courting couple. But it is in *Lechery* that Brueghel gives free-est play to his imagination. Elaborate tree arbours, hollow treetrunks and an extraordinary treehouse shaped like a giant clamshell all play host to the most unimaginable and improbable goings-on.

The Dutch artist Hieronymus Bosch's triptych *The Garden of Earthly Delights*, painted between 1485 and 1510, depicts a man as a tree, and his broken egg-shaped body, supported on trunk-like legs, houses a kind of forlorn tavern where solemn nudes sit stiffly waiting for a servant to draw their wine.

This is a frightening, allegorical picture, full of demons and lost souls awaiting their descent into Hell.

English Treehouses

In Tudor England 'roosting places', as treehouses were then known, were an essential part of garden decoration. These shady arbours were particularly enjoyed by the ladies of the household as summertime retreats in which to work at their embroidery and to gossip.

Lime trees would often be meticulously pruned and shaped to create natural chambers rising in tiers through the tree. The roofs and walls were formed by bending and intertwining the branches downwards. Across the floors of each tier, planks would be laid.

A treehouse like this existed for many years at Cobham Hall, near Rochester in Kent. John Parkinson describes it in his *Paradiso in Sole* in 1629, explaining how lime trees were planted to provide '. . . goodly arbours and summer banqueting houses – either on the ground, the boughs serving very handsomely to plash round about it', or higher up in a second arbour, or even a third above that.

He goes on: 'I have seen at Cobham a tall lime tree, bare without branches for 8 foot and then the branches spread round so orderly as if it were done by art and brought to compass the middle arbour.' Above that the trunk was bare for another eight or nine feet with the higher branches bent down to make a second arbour, 'wherein might bee placed halfe a hundred men at the least, as there might be likewise in that underneath'. Higher still another row of branches were bent to create a third arbour. He describes how planks were laid on the boughs to tread upon. This was '. . . the goodliest spectacle mine eyes ever beheld for one tree to carry'. John Parkinson was so enamoured of this treehouse at Cobham Hall that he mentions it again in his *Theatrum Botanicum* (1640), referring to a '. . . remarkable three-storied, pleached, lime bower, which served as a banquet house there at Cobham'.

After the publication of *Paradiso in Sole* and *Paradisus Terestris*, Charles I gave Parkinson the title of '*Botanicus*

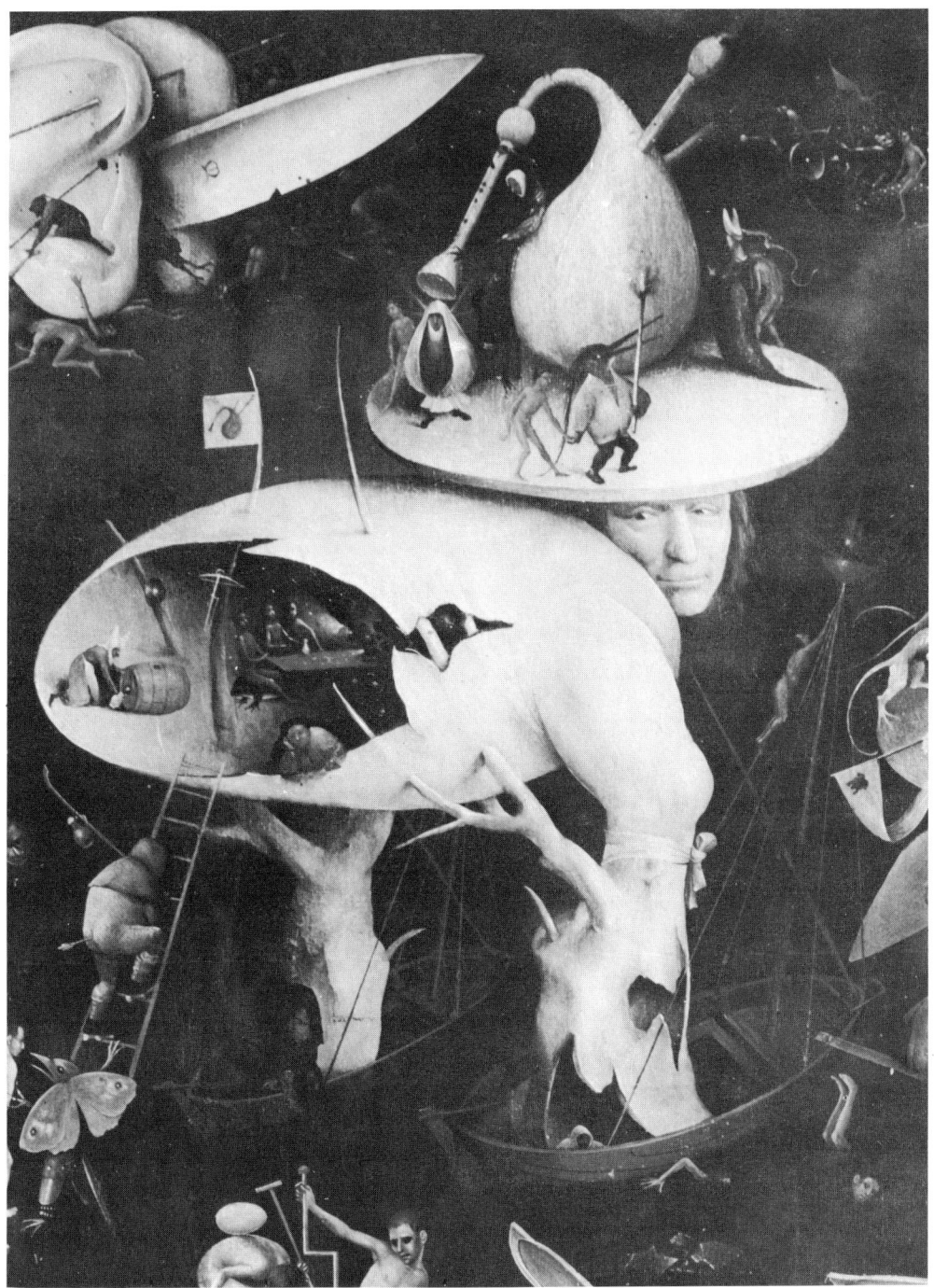

The Treeman – a detail from Hieronymus Bosch's The Garden of Earthly Delights

Regius Primarius' – 'The King's Chief Botanist'.

Queen Elizabeth I stayed at Cobham during one of her royal progresses round the country, and by all accounts she enjoyed the famous treehouse very much indeed. Holinshed mentions this visit in one of his chronicles: 'A banqueting hall made for her Majesty in Cobham Park with a goodly gallery, thereunto, composed all of green, with several devices of knotted flowers . . . which nature seemed to have planted there of purpose in summer time to welcome her Majesty and to honour their Lord and Master.' Sadly no court photographer was present to record the scene. Reluctantly Holinshed concludes, 'But because the beauty and majesty, with the rare device thereof

The treehouse at Cobham Hall where Queen Elizabeth I banqueted among the branches

From John Evelyn's sketch of his treehouse at Wotton in Surrey in 1646. Note the domed pavilion. Has a more elegant treehouse ever been created?

cannot be so well conceived by pen as the same was artificially made, unless the reader might at one instant behold also the artificial situation of the place, I think it better to pass . . .'

John Evelyn the famous diarist of the seventeenth century would certainly have seen Lord Cobham's famous treehouse. Evelyn was interested in all aspects of gardening and forestry and wrote several treatises, including his *Silva*. He too decided to build a treehouse.

A drawing of his at Christ Church College, Oxford, dated 1646, shows his garden designs including the treehouse. There is a tall tree with a stepway leading up to a balustraded platform built around the tree and partly supported on tall poles at the corners. On the platform is a small pavilion with a domed cupola.

A Victorian treehouse bower. Coleridge wrote of his own bower, 'Friendship is a sheltering tree'

With a few notable exceptions, in Britain the fashion for treehouses disappeared almost entirely during the Victorian era. Arbours and pergolas became rather more popular.

The poet Coleridge had a lime bower in his garden in Somerset. Charles Lamb paid him a visit in 1797 on the very day when he had scalded his foot and could not get about.

Instead he remained confined to his bower and composed the poem 'This Lime Bower my Prison': 'Here must I remain, this lime bower my prison.' But it was Coleridge who also wrote 'Friendship is a sheltering tree.'

Renaissance in the New World

Just as the tradition of treehouses was fading in Europe, an enterprising American took the idea to Philadelphia. In the late eighteenth century soon after the American War of Independence, landowner Mr John Ross created a 'Medici' style roost in his estate at Haverford. A keen silviculturist he designed a shady tree walk nearly a mile long overhung by tall forest trees and near the beginning he built a seat some twelve feet up in the trees. According to his granddaughter's description this 'seat' was capable of holding upwards of twenty people with space for a large table. On the Fourth of July, patriotic John Ross flew the Stars and Stripes from a nearby flagstaff and celebrated the day with friends up in the treehouse, where iced wine would be served. Treehouse entertaining became such a popular pastime in Haverford that it was extended to many a warm summer day. John Ross even installed a bell wire connecting with his house in order to call his servant when required, 'and avoid his constant presence'.

During the nineteenth century, when Wordsworth and Tennyson were proclaiming the splendours of nature, hollow trees were popular venues for outings and picnics. The Rosemaund Oak, in Herefordshire, and the Major Oak, in Sherwood Forest, became famous during these years.

But perhaps most surprising of all is the fact that the Queen who gave her name to this period had as thirteen-year-old Princess Victoria, visited and sketched in a 'House in a Tree' at Pitchford Hall, in the heart of England, a treehouse that had been built 400 years earlier and which stands there still to this very day.

The treehouse looking towards Pitchford Hall. Both the hall and the treehouse date from the sixteenth century

Stately Treehouses, Old and New

Pitchford Hall

An Ordnance Survey map of the Shrewsbury area (grid reference 3528. 3043) shows just to the south of Pitchford Hall (now owned by Caroline Colthurst) a bushy-topped tree with the words 'The tree with a house in it'. One wonders if there are any other treehouses anywhere in the world actually marked on a Government map! It has a further claim to fame: on 2 May 1977 it was declared a Grade I Listed Historic Building. Official recognition never comes easily or quickly, but by any stretch of the imagination it is amazing that a treehouse built during the reign of Queen Elizabeth I should survive in the branches of the same lime tree for more than 450 years, spanning the reigns of fifteen monarchs, to gain its architectural seal of approval during the Silver Jubilee year of Queen Elizabeth II.

References to this treehouse are many and varied, but they are easy to miss, since for most people living nearby Pitchford Hall has the greater claim to fame. It is described in the pamphlet of the local parish church at Acton Burnel as the 'finest timber-framed house in Shropshire'. Half hidden in the same paragraph is the sentence, 'There is a timber-framed summerhouse in a great lime tree in the garden.' The Society for the Protection of Ancient Buildings does it more justice. After a description of the Hall, it concludes: 'Opposite the south front, up the hill is the enchanting folly of a timber-framed Summer House in the branches of a tree. It has the prettiest Gothick decoration. . . .'

There has been a manor house at Pitchford since before the Conquest. In the subsequent re-distribution of land, it became the property of a Norman knight whose family lived there for many generations. The tiny church just to the north of Pitchford Hall, with its pretty weatherboarded pyramidal belfry, contains ample evidence of Norman design: there is a blocked window in the north wall with herringbone masonry below and a rounded, unmoulded doorway on the north side of the chancel. The church contains a wooden effigy of John de Pitchford, 1285, and there are excellently drawn incised alabaster memorial slabs of the Pitchford family, the most recent date being 1587. By then, however, the Hall had been purchased and rebuilt by a family of wool merchants from Shrewsbury. It was this family who created the treehouse.

Thomas Ottley bought Pitchford Hall in 1473, but although he started the rebuilding, it was not for another two generations of Ottleys that the present timber-framed Hall was completed in 1549. The treehouse was most probably constructed at some time during the next fifty years.

The treehouse was first depicted on a map of the house and grounds drawn by a John Boiven and dated 1714. His map is a sort of bird's eye view with the house surrounded by bushy-topped trees in one of which stands the exact replica of the timber-and-plaster treehouse still existing today.

At first glance, what strikes a visitor to Pitchford is that, despite the impressive size of the Hall, it has a very homely aspect. There is plentiful use of diagonal struts, but the framing is not too ornate, and the Hall has the appearance of an oversized cottage with two projecting wings. The tiled roof is sparred with enchanting 'Hampton Court' star-shaped chimneystacks. The summerhouse built in the branches of a great lime tree at the top of a rise to the south of the Hall, and close by the pretty orangery, is of a similar design. It is not so much a treehouse as a Tudor house in a tree.

Shropshire County Council Sites and Monuments Records state: 'SA 13351. Post Medieval. Type Gazebo. Probably early C17, altered and enriched in mid C18. Single celled structure approx. 10 c.ft. in a large lime tree on an eminence in the grounds of Pitchford Hall. About 11 ft. off the ground and reached by a timber staircase. An ogeeheaded aperture in each wall. A door and three windows.'

One may wonder what prompted a practical, hard-headed wool merchant to construct such an elaborate treehouse. Admittedly this period was the 'golden age' of treehouses. The

Stately Treehouses, Old and New

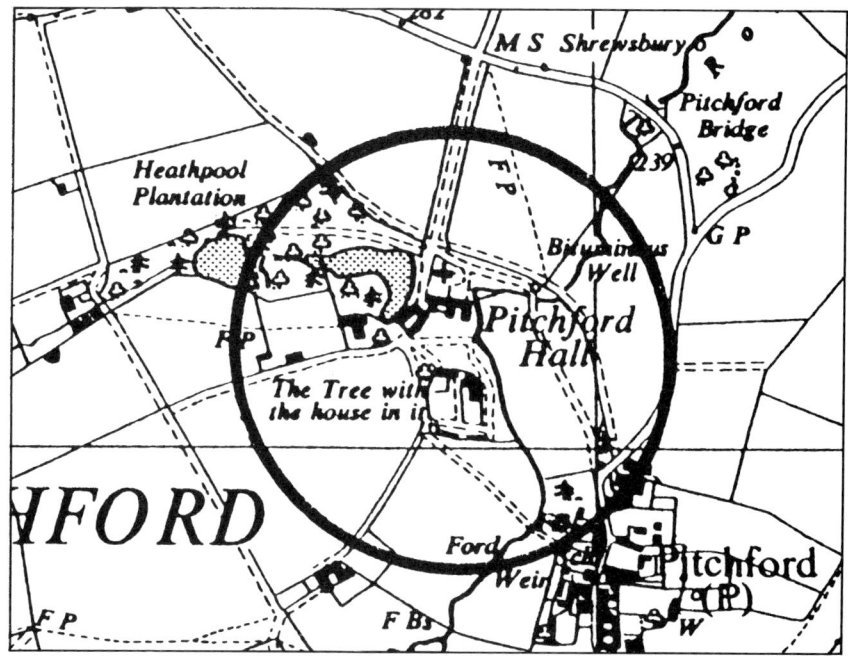

An Ordnance Survey map showing Pitchford Hall. Surely this is the only Government map in the world listing 'House in a Tree'?

Ottleys may not have read John Parkinson's *Paradiso in Sole* or the travels of Fynnes Morrison, but they would probably have been well aware of the latest fashions in landscape gardening. Even so, as we have seen, Elizabethan treehouses were almost exclusively arbours, not houses in trees.

Perhaps as remarkable as the house itself was the choice of tree. Lime trees, with their sweeping pendulous branches, may make splendid arbours but the common small-leafed English lime, *Tilia Cordata*, has a limited lifespan. It rarely lives as long as an oak. Was it luck or foresight that prompted the Ottleys to select a mature specimen of *Tilia Platyphillos*, the larger-leafed and longer-living lime, in which to build their summerhouse?

Although this particular species of lime is widespread in Europe, there are relatively few examples in England. Some that were planted before 1600 are still alive, such as the celebrated tree at Burghley, near Stamford, planted by Queen Elizabeth I. Lime trees of this species are usually isolated trees growing best in open parkland. Sturdy and robust, they can withstand the full force of wind and gales and more insidious enemies such as frost, drought and decay. *Tilia Platyphillos* can live for more than a thousand years, although when the Ottleys decided to put their summerhouse in the branches of an already old lime tree, they could hardly have imagined that it would have lasted even one century, let alone nearly five.

Unfortunately, records of its original construction have long since been lost. Probably the costs were absorbed into the household or the estate accounts – the shillings and sixpences to pay the carpenters and tilers were simply ascribed to general handymen's wages. On the other hand, craftsmen in those days built things to last. The oak beams used for the timber frame, and the supporting raft it was fixed to, would have been of the same seasoned quality as those used in the building of the Hall itself.

Succeeding generations of Ottleys took particular pride in their 'House in the Tree'. Set on the crest of a rise, it commands sweeping views south and west towards the steep bald slopes of the Long Mynd and the distant blue Welsh hills. Ottleys of all ages must have spent many a pleasant hour here. It served as a playhouse for children, and rendezvous for courting couples and a safe haven from the worries of commerce and politics. The burghers of the fifteenth century became the squires of the seventeenth, and during the Civil War Sir Francis Ottley was Governor of Shrewsbury.

In the latter half of the eighteenth century the treehouse underwent its first major reconstruction, updated in keeping with the style of the period. The windows and door frames were rebuilt with ogee headings; inside, the plasterwork was intricately enriched to create rococo-Gothick motifs, clustered shafts at the corners and a frieze of alternating lozenges and quatrefoils supporting covings with pointed arches. Looking down from the centre of the ceiling is a female mask with rays extending from it.

The redecoration was done with all the artisan skill and quality that made English craftsmanship of that era so famous around the world. It may seem strange to us now that a mere treehouse should receive the exact same care and lavish attention that went into building of the great country house but things were built to last in those days, and the magnificent decorations have remained virtually unimpaired up to the present day.

It was during this period that the original exterior timber frame was plastered over, the rendering being done in such a way as to simulate stone. No longer was it just a flimsy construction in a tree; it had every appearance of a stone house. This was the great age of follies, and what better example than the illusion of a masonry building in the boughs of a lime tree. One can imagine how visitors must have gasped in surprise, wondering for a moment if their own senses were deceiving them and if what they were seeing for the first time was no more than a *trompe l'œil* – a trick of the eye!

Finally, after thirteen generations, the Ottley family died out through lack of heirs, and the Hall passed to a distant cousin – the half-brother of the Earl of Liverpool. He had three sons and a daughter, Louisa, to whom he left Pitchford.

Louisa was a maid of honour at Queen Victoria's Coronation, their friendship having been established several years earlier when the then Princess Victoria came to Pitchford for a visit, when by all accounts, the future Queen was definitely 'amused'.

The year was 1832 and the Princess was thirteen years old. For some time she had been travelling around Britain to see her future realm. She arrived at Pitchford Hall on 27 October, and wrote in her diary: 'At about 20 minutes to 5 we arrived at Pitchford, a curious looking but very comfortable house. It is striped black and white and in the shape of a cottage. We dined at ½ past 6. After dinner 2 young ladies, Lady Salina and Lady Louise played on harp and piano. I stayed up till ½ past 8. I was soon in bed and asleep.'

During supper someone must have mentioned the treehouse, because that was one of the things Victoria wanted to see next day. Unfortunately it was a Sunday, when pious duty came first: 'Sunday October 28th. I awoke at 7 and got up at ½ past 7. At ½ past 9 we breakfasted. After breakfast I drew and at 11 we went to church. At a little past one we came home and walked about the grounds, and I went up a staircase to a little house in a tree.'

Princess Victoria remained at Pitchford until 3 November. She visited the treehouse on several more occasions with Louisa, chatting and drawing pretty sketches, and it was from there that she watched the local hunt ride by.

A hundred years passed before the next royal visit occurred, when George V and Queen Mary went to Pitchford, and in

An interior view of Pitchford treehouse. The fine Chippendale plasterwork has helped make this treehouse a listed architectural building

April 1935 the future George VI and Queen Elizabeth stayed there.

By the time King George and Queen Mary paid their visit, the Hall had passed on to Lady Sybil Grant. The daughter of the first Earl of Rosebery and his wife Hannah Rothschild, Sybil married Sir Charles Grant, the owner of Pitchford Hall, and inherited the property on his death.

Lady Sybil Grant was not only a very eccentric person but took a special interest in the treehouse. In fact, she virtually lived in it. The present owner, Caroline Colthurst, is the step-daughter of Lady Sybil's son Robin Grant, and to her we owe a description of some of Lady Sybil's oddities.

Sybil Grant could not bear the sound of running water. It so happens that the brook which flows through the estate passes just beneath the bedroom windows on the east wing of the Hall. There is even a low weir at this point. To Lady Sybil the noise was intolerable and she moved out of the Hall and into the Orangery close by the treehouse. It was this, more than anything else, that established the locally held opinion that she was a witch.

'Witches', Caroline Colthurst assured me, 'hate the sound of running water.'

Quite apart from this unusual phobia, Lady Sybil indulged in other activities which people regarded as odd and which encouraged gossip. For a start, her appearance: the older she got, the fatter she became. To say she was extremely large would be an understatement. Added to this, she dyed her hair with henna to a brilliant orange hue and was constantly surrounded by a pack of dogs, who even shared her four-poster bed.

She spent a great deal of her time in the treehouse. Here she worked at her embroidery and told the fortune of anyone who was prepared to cross her palm with sufficient silver. (It would be fair to say that during this time her only friends were the gypsies.)

In addition to Pitchford Hall, the Grants had a house on the Epsom Downs and one in Scotland. Lady Sybil travelled between them in a converted horsebox towed by a Rolls Royce driven by the family chauffeur. Each night they would stop at an inn. After dinner the chauffeur slept in the inn while Lady Sybil held court in the horsebox, telling the fortunes of those she regarded with favour.

The result of all this was that, for many years between the wars, it was claimed that Pitchford Hall was ruled by a witch who lived in a treehouse and cast spells on anyone she disliked.

Rather sadly, one of her strongest dislikes was reserved for her own son. Robin Grant joined the Navy and rose to the rank of Commander, but Sybil disapproved of his first marriage and disinherited him, leaving Pitchford Hall to the National Library of Wales. Fortunately for the family, the Will was couched in rather ambiguous terms. In fact, all that was left to the National Library were the four walls and roof – no contents, no land, nothing, so Sir Robin Grant was able to buy back the shell of Pitchford Hall. Even the ghosts stayed put.

According to Caroline Colthurst, there are five ghosts, the most common being a tobacco-smelling ghost whom she thinks must be her stepfather. 'There's something salty about it too,' she chuckled. 'Still, the ghosts are good for the tourists. The Americans love to stay in haunted houses.'

Pitchford Hall is on the Stately Homes 'Bed and Breakfast' list, and a more splendid place to stay in and sample the atmosphere of Olde Worlde England would be hard to imagine. The treehouse is very popular with courting couples, says Mrs Colthurst, recalling a tenant of hers in the village who was much attracted to a friend staying at the Hall. Both of them were too reserved to say anything to the other, so Caroline arranged a tea-party in the treehouse, dragging up an old mattress for the children to sit on. The tenant and the guest were also invited – no one else. She laughed. 'After tea the children came home, but we didn't see the happy pair for days!'

One doubts if it was the first time in its long history that the treehouse had played host to young love.

The treehouse would never have continued to host anyone at all if Mrs Colthurst had not decided to go ahead with much-needed repairs. When she inherited the Hall in 1972, the treehouse was suffering from years of neglect, and the old lime tree itself was in a fairly parlous condition. Unfortunately her immediate problem was enormous death duties. The treehouse had to wait.

It waited until a severe gale in 1977 almost demolished it in a single day. The *Birmingham Post* of 7 December 1977 reported: '... during last month's gales both tree and house began to sway like a sailor three sheets in the wind!'

By then tree and treehouse were in a truly sorry state. The great limbs of the lime were half rotted, the trunk was hollow, the boughs were propped up with timber posts and breeze blocks. As for the treehouse, the oak raft on which it stood was partly rotted away, the oak beams of the house itself were ravaged by beetle, and the fine seventeenth-century plaster ceiling was cracking and crumbling every time the tree creaked in the wind. Every fresh storm wreaked more havoc.

The Colthursts realized that something had to be done urgently. They turned to architect Rodney Melville for advice. In a letter to Shrewsbury and Atchum Borough Council, Melville identified the problem:

1. The house is partly supported by the tree and partly on a variety of timber posts or lightweight concrete block piers. Movement and decay of the tree coupled with differential movement in the posts is causing the very fine 18th century internal plasterwork to break up.
2. The flimsy timber frame, which was never meant to be exposed to the weather and was until earlier this century protected by rendering, is decaying under the combined onslaught of beetle attack and wet rot.

Rodney Melville decided to call in a firm of structural engineers to advise on the best course of action. He invited the London-based firm of John Mason Ltd to recommend the best way to support the treehouse once the tree had been restored.

Caroline Colthurst explained, 'You see, it had never been looked at as an engineering problem before. People had just propped it up.'

The tree surgery was done by T. Mousley & Sons, whose list of suggestions filled several pages. There was the dead wood to be cut away, wounds to be pasted with a fungicide sealant, large holes to be covered with plastic sheeting, which in turn was protected by lead or zinc tacked to the limb and coloured for camouflage. In other places drain plugs had to be drilled through to drain off any moisture that collected.

The tree surgeons then turned their attention to the three main limbs and decided they must be '... braced together using 6mm high tensile steel wire attached to ½ inch eyebolts fitted through the limbs...' They recommended steel props to support the major limbs, and finally observed: 'Because of rabbit infestation of the tree's roots we recommend a protective fence all round at 6 metres distant from the trunk.'

The estimate for the tree surgery alone came to £800. In the event some of these proposals such as the rabbit fence, were not taken up, and the great old limbs are supported only by slender metal poles. As a result, unlike the Major Oak in Sherwood Forest, which looks as if it would collapse without its massive props, the great lime at Pitchford has a jaunty, confident air about it. Possibly rabbits still nibble the roots but the tree does not seem to be affected. Perhaps the bunches of mistletoe hanging from the boughs have conferred their pagan magical powers of potency.

The structural work on the treehouse was undertaken by Henry Willock & Sons. A steel frame was inserted under it, and this was supported by four tubular steel columns carefully concealed. Once these were in place, the treehouse was held up independently from the tree. The lime might creak and sway in the autumn gales, but no longer could the strains and stresses damage the treehouse itself.

Skilled craftsmen were required to repair and replace the oak frame timbers and to restore the plasterwork to its former glory. Two carpenters from the nearby village of Crosshouses began work on the wood, and a member of the Federation of Master Builders from Shrewsbury was chosen to undertake the replastering. It was a task that was to keep them busy in the treehouse for several months.

The final bill came to £14,678.49. It is interesting to speculate what would have been the original cost of building the treehouse in the first place – probably no more than a few pounds.

There was also another decision to be taken: how to plaster the outside, whether to leave the black timber frames showing or to cover them up. Prints of a hundred years earlier depicted the plaster dabbed on so as to simulate stone. In a letter to Mrs Colthurst, Rodney Melville wrote: 'Whilst the Treehouse in its present (timber frame) form is very striking, the image of a masonry structure placed in a tree is much stronger by virtue of the obvious illogicality of the decision and the conscious effort to deceive.'

'It was up to us and the HBC,' Mrs Colthurst explained. 'We decided to keep the old timber framework.'

Stately Treehouses, Old and New

An eighteenth-century view of the treehouse clad in stucco

The Historic Buildings Council, which comes under the auspices of the Department of the Environment, was brought into the restoration project at an early stage. The treehouse was declared a listed buildings, but only after protracted negotiations was a grant awarded towards the cost of the repairs. The grant was subject to certain conditions. The Historic Buildings Council declared: 'Nevertheless it is essential that the taxpayer should derive some direct benefit from the grants and that it should be made as easy as possible for him to see how his money has been spent . . .'

Mrs Colthurst – for whom her home was her castle in a more literal sense than applies to most of us – was not to be easily intimidated: 'You will appreciate that problems could arise regarding the question of access to the Tree House . . . We do not want a lot of strangers wandering about in the vicinity of the House as there is the question of security. I am sure some satisfactory formula can be worked out . . .'

There was. HBC wrote back with the suggestion: 'That members of the public will be allowed to have access to the interior of the Treehouse by appointment throughout the year and that adequate publicity is given to this arrangement.' The HBC even had the tongue-in-cheek courtesy to conclude: 'I will be grateful if you could let me know whether you are now able to accept the offer of a grant.'

The lady was prepared to accept, although it was not until four years later that a cheque for £5,000 finally arrived. By then the treehouse had long since been returned to its former splendid state. On 24 May 1980 Sir Peter Gadsden, the Lord Mayor of London, had ceremonially declared the treehouse restored. He even planted a tree to mark the occasion – not a *Tilia Platyphyllos*, but a *Salix Caprea Pendula* (for simple country-lovers, a common willow).

After Mrs Colthurst had shown me round the treehouse, we returned via the Orangery to the Hall, where an American family were gazing about them in bewilderment. 'Can you imagine actually living here?' one of them said amazed. I could appreciate their delight. I had experienced the same feeling the moment I first glimpsed Pitchford Hall.

As Mrs Colthurst showed me out, she gave me a brochure. 'The ghosts are all thrown in for free,' she said, adding with a wink, 'but if you want a mattress up in the treehouse, that's extra!'

Plas Newydd

In 1975 the seventh Marquess of Anglesey had a treehouse built in the grounds of Plas Newydd, his ancestral home on the Isle of Anglesey, as a present for his daughter, Lady Amelia Paget's twelfth birthday.

The Paget estate at Plas Newydd lies along the sheltered eastern coast of the Isle of Anglesey, overlooking the Menai Strait. Protected from the gales that blast across the Irish Sea, warmed by the Gulf Stream with its spectacular view over the Strait to the mountains of Snowdonia, Plas Newydd is situated in a most favourable and attractive place. Spring comes early here, frosts are rare, and the combination of fertile soil and a moist atmosphere makes this part of the Anglesey coast a haven for exotic plants and shrubs, especially rhododendrons. Trees grow tall here, and the woods contain oaks, sycamores and pines of great age and remarkable girth.

The Paget family have been at Plas Newydd a long time. They span a great deal of British history, and it is perhaps appropriate that the present Marquess is himself a military historian.

The Pagets came to Plas Newydd through marriage. In the early years of the fifteenth century Gwilym ap Griffith, head of a powerful local family, married Morfed Tudur, whose uncle was great-grandfather to Henry VII. From this marriage Gwilym acquired considerable properties in the Isle of Anglesey, including Plas Newydd (New Place), an estate on the coast of the Menai Strait. His descendants built the original house here early in the sixteenth century.

The first Baron Paget had been one of Henry VIII's chief advisers and an executor of his Will. In the course of succeeding centuries, some Pagets gained renown as soldiers and statesmen, others were best remembered for their eccentricities. Perhaps there was none more famous than the tenth Baron Paget. During the Flanders campaign of 1799 he had served under the notable Duke of York and later, during the Peninsular Wars, with only a small cavalry force he successfully screened the British retreat to Corunna. At Waterloo he was Wellington's aide-de-camp, and afterwards he was created Marquess of Anglesey for his bravery. It was while he was surveying the battlefield on horseback with the Iron Duke that grapeshot blew off his leg. Looking down, he is reputed to have exclaimed, 'By God, sir, I've lost my leg!' The Duke, momentarily removing his spy-glass, replied, 'By God, sir, so you have!' At this both resumed their survey of the retreating French. The leg was buried with full military honours, and the Marquess, who recovered amazingly quickly, was fitted with one of the first articulated wooden legs, later known as 'the Anglesey Leg'. An example of this remains to this day at Plas Newydd. In 1828 he became Lord Lieutenant of Ireland.

In building the treehouse, the seventh Marquess was merely adding another folly in line with the many alterations in the long history of the house and gardens. Sir Nicholas Bayly (who married the eighth Lord Paget's daughter Caroline and took over the estate) constructed a semi-circular turret in the middle of the east front, and an octagonal tower at the south-east corner. In this present century the sixth Marquess, who redesigned the entire house, commissioned Rex Whistler to paint scenic views in the remodelled dining-room: brilliant perspective vistas through colonnades across a harbour scene to renaissance cities with buildings of every period and style jostling each other on the quaysides. These pastiches are as delightful as they are amusing. The entire Anglesey family is seen in a gondola; the Marquess's father is depicted under the hoofs of Marcus Aurelius's horse; the steeple of St Martin-in-the-Fields, Trajan's Column and a triumphal arch with an inscription commemorating the founding of the city by the Paget family are all included. These incredible canvases are universally regarded as masterpieces of *trompe l'œil* painting.

The sixth Marquess inherited Plas Newydd from his cousin, the fifth Marquess, a notable eccentric whose hobbies included running his own theatrical company. He converted the chapel into a theatre to stage the productions, with himself very often as the sole audience. In winter he ordered that hundreds of braziers be kept burning night and day along the woodland paths in case he wanted to warm himself while out walking. Once he is reputed to have thrown a bejewelled fur coat worth thousands of pounds into one of the fires simply because he felt too hot!

Planning Lady Amelia's birthday gift the present Marquess, together with the Estate Forestry Department, chose a tree with a large 'saddle' on which to rest the structure. It was built like a log cabin, with split pine trunks nailed together, and a timber plank floor. The room inside is about four feet by five, and there is a ladder with a handrail leading from the open doorway to the ground below.

In 1976, the year after Lady Amelia's treehouse was built, the Marquess gave Plas Newydd and much of the estate along the Menai Strait to the National Trust, though he still lives in part of the house. Even if it was only a parting gesture, his illustrious ancestors would surely have unreservedly approved of his adding, not only for his daughter's pleasure but for visiting children of all ages from then on, the attraction of a log cabin up in a lime tree.

Belton House

Belton House is set in landscaped parkland among the low, rolling downland of east Lincolnshire, twenty-five miles inland from the Wash and a few miles north of the market town of Grantham.

The house is a fine example of Restoration architecture. Completed in 1688 for Sir John Brownlow, it possesses a grandeur reminiscent of Versailles. Behind the symmetrical

Belton House Adventure Park. A Lilliputian wonderland of treehouses and treewalks

H-planned building lies the formal nineteenth century garden with its beautiful orangery designed by Jeffrey Wyatville.

Treehouses seem a far cry from this stylized landscaping. In fact, the treehouses at Belton are very recent additions, developed since the National Trust took over the property. To find them, one must leave the great park with its breathtaking avenue of trees leading to the Belmont Tower, cross a stone bridge over a weir and enter a forest of Californian redwood trees with soaring trunks and slender pyramidal crowns. Mixed among the redwoods are giant beech trees. A miniature steam railway packed with delighted youngsters chugs through the undergrowth below, while on all sides, suspended fifteen to twenty feet up in the air is the most amazing assortment of treehouses: treeforts, treewalks, ropeways suspended from the branches, ropes dangling from treehouse doorways for the adventurous to haul themselves up or slide down; ropeladders, stepladders, parapets abound. The split pinelog walls nailed vertically on the treehouse frames create a

Fort Alamo at Belton Park, where youngsters of all ages can indulge their pioneering fantasies

frontier atmosphere of forts and watchtowers. It is reminiscent of the Wild West, Davy Crockett and the Alamo all in one.

The only mildly alarming feature in this whole complex set up in the trees and swarming with boisterous children is that it is exclusively a Lilliputian world where anyone over four feet feels like a hopelessly oversized Gulliver. However, if the intention was to inspire a new generation of treehouse-lovers, no stately home garden could have been put to better use – especially since Belton House is only a twenty-minute drive from the heart of Sherwood Forest, whose famous legends from time immemorial have inspired children of all generations to play at Robin Hood and his Merry Men in every hollow oak tree available.

In a way it is a pity that there are no equivalent treehouses and treewalks for adults at Belton House. Marvellous as it is, the Adventure Park emphasizes the attitude that treehouse are playpens for children. While the youngsters shriek happily among the treetops and their parents wait patiently below, one feels a sense of loss for the past grandeur of the wonderful Renaissance treehouses at Pratolino and Castello, Schaffhausen and Cobham Hall, and of envy for the Japanese enjoying their stylized treewalks at Kyoto. Thankful as one must be to the National Trust for encouraging the treehouse idea, even they were rather condescending when their Regional Office wrote to me, 'I fear your forthcoming book on treehouses may be a slim one.'

The West Country

At the River Dart Country Park in glorious Devon, Patrick Simpson, the Managing Director, maintains a proprietorial eye over the two treehouses in the grounds which also include other adventure attractions for the energetic, such as Tarzan swings, and a rope bridge over the river. He gives the following tongue-in-cheek description:

> These are first floor dwellings, each having one reception/living area, with all round woodland and lakeside views. Situated twixt oak and ash, with no neighbouring properties visible, yet facilities within easy walking distance.
>
> Suitable access is given through the floor in both cases with the exit door conveniently placed beside a Fireman's Pole in one case

and a knotted rope in the other.

Both properties are most soundly built, being 11 years old and still in first-class condition. They are walled and roofed with bark-covered offcuts and adequate ventilation is given through the all round windows, which as yet, have no glass in them. Plumbing is of the natural variety and operated by gravity on a one-way system.

The immense popularity of these houses over the last 11 years has resulted in what is probably the greatest turnover of occupancy rate, of any treehouses world wide, with an estimated occupancy for summer rate only, of 50,000 persons each, per year.

Heale House

The Woodford Valley seems at times almost an enchanted place as it winds slowly south out of the Salisbury Plain, lush with hanging beechwoods, paddocks and old dovecoted manor houses. The River Avon, at this point little more than an overgrown stream, rushes beside the road and through the gardens of the thatched cottages of Great Durnford and Upper Woodford. Ten miles to the south, at Salisbury, it will receive the tributaries of the Wyle, the Nadder and the Bourne, flowing in from all points of the compass, but in the quiet Woodford valley it is still a chattering stream, passing cow meadows, woods and sheepfolds, and the grounds of Heale House.

Heale House and its eight acres of garden lie beside the river at Middle Woodford, and much of the house remains unchanged since those hectic days when King Charles II sheltered here after the Battle of Worcester in 1651. In the words of Arthur Bryant, 'at nightfall they found the welcoming lights of Heale House.' Nowadays high clipped hedges screen the house from the road. Only the rooftops are visible across the meadows. An avenue of horse-chestnuts winds round to it. Behind the hedges ornamental stepped terraces slope down to the house, and lawns slip away on either side to the river.

The gardens, however, are very different from what they were then. The clue or the culprit is the river, for without the river there would never have been a water-garden created, and it is on the banks of one of the tributary streams that the treehouse stands — a treehouse inside the hollow bole of an immense and ancient elm tree.

The water-garden resembles a painting on a willow-pattern

The treehouse at Heale House was originally a hollow elm tree. It stands beside and rather aloof from the famous Japanese water gardens

plate. A red-painted *nikko* bridge crosses to an ornamental island, and weeping willows overhang the stream, bordered by acers and magnolias. A pagoda-roofed tea-house with sliding paper screens is poised over the water. Bamboos, stone lanterns, irises and a rare Cercidiphyllum Japonicum (a symbol of unified love) all combine to create the effect of a perfect imitation landscape. One has the feeling of stepping into another world.

Lady Anne Rasch, the present owner, explained how it came into being. Her grandfather – the Hon. Louis Greville, younger son of the Earl of Warwick, had bought Heale House in 1894. It was at this period that the culture of Japan first excited Western imagination and when in 1901 he returned from Diplomatic Service in Japan, he brought back not only the thatched tea-house but four Japanese gardeners to create the authentic water-garden. From the teahouse we turned our attention to the treehouse – looking rather out of place in the skilfully crafted garden – a huge, knobbly and totally dead bole of an elm tree.

Lady Anne smiled at my enquiry. 'It was Guy's, my son's treehouse. It must have been hollow for centuries. He used to climb down into it through the hole in the top. The trunk baffled all sounds. Once inside he could hide as long as he wanted. We made the little door as an escape hatch.'

The door, once closed, was almost invisible, as it was made out of the treetrunk itself, bark and all.

'It's fun, isn't it?' Lady Anne said. 'Children love it. The tree was alive until the elm disease killed it. It must be six or seven hundred years old at least.'

This immediately set me wondering who else may have used the hollow elm tree during the centuries it has stood at Heale House. Lady Anne must have guessed what I was thinking for she laughed. 'I'm sure it was hollow when King Charles sheltered at the house after the Battle of Worcester. They hid him in a priest's hole. I daresay he'd had enough of hiding in trees by then.'

Chartwell
Winston Churchill purchased Chartwell in 1924. Originally a Tudor manor and later developed into a comfortable modern house close to the village of Westerham, it stands just below the crest of the North Downs with magnificent sweeping

'Cuckoo!' A cartoon from the Daily Express *shortly after Budget Day 1927, the year Churchill built his treehouse*

views south over the Weald of Kent.

The front of the house is flanked by two giant lime trees. The right-hand one stands beside the gravel drive, and it was in the branches of this tree that Churchill built a house for his children soon after they moved to Chartwell.

Trees may have been rather in his mind at this period, for these were the years when he was Chancellor of the Exchequer in Baldwin's Government, and the political cartoons of the time lampooned him as a mighty axeman hacking his way through forests of 'Waste', 'Expenditure' and 'Extravagance' (*Leeds Mercury*). There are many cartoons of this nature and they can be found in the archives of the Churchill College Library at Cambridge. The archivist will produce on request enormous files of press cuttings and photographs. There are pictures of Churchill tiling a roof, making a snowman and building a wall but unfortunately none of the treehouse.

A *Daily Express* cartoon of 29 March 1927 entitled

'Cuckoo' depicts Churchill as a rather racy 'bird' labelled 'Budget', perched on the treetops and surveying through a telescope a series of nests occupied by frightened top-hatted City gentlemen. The woodland theme continues in a cartoon entitled 'Little Red Riding Hood and the Wolf'. Churchill as the wolf hides behind a bush awaiting 'Little Red Riding Hood' clutching a bag laden with 'Wine' and 'Tobacco'.

Perhaps all this is mere speculation, but the fact remains that long before Churchill started his hobby of bricklaying and creating that final, enduring example of his craft, the Wendy House, constructed for his youngest daughter, Mary, he set about building a treehouse in the great lime.

As a model he would have had *The Swiss Family Robinson*'s account to go on. In that book, the treehouse, with its ladder which could be raised up for security, was aptly described as 'a Castle in the Air'. Perhaps he had this in mind, for it was a substantial structure he created.

Although he originally built the treehouse for his children, Churchill often frequented it himself. He liked trees and as a young man, while staying at Salisbury Hall in Hertfordshire with his mother and stepfather, George Cornwallis-West, he often composed speeches while sitting up in the branches of his favourite tree. He referred to it as his 'aerial study', and it was here that he wrote some of his most vitriolic compositions. Local legend has it that, as the pages fluttered to the ground, they scorched the grass.

Sadly, as with so many things subject to the vagaries of weather and time, bar a few rusty nails, little trace of the treehouse remains at Chartwell. For a first-hand account of it we rely on Sarah Churchill's book *A Thread in the Tapestry*: 'My father had built a house in the lime tree for his children. It was a two-storeyed affair: it was a good twenty feet high and was reached by first shinning up a rope and then climbing on carefully placed struts between four stems of the elm [lime]. Pebbin [her cousin Peregrine] and I inherited when we were old enough to climb it. Our privacy was strongly protected as my father placed a special cross-bar half way up the tree and this stopped anyone bigger than ourselves climbing any further.' Only the lime tree remains.

The gardens of Plas Newydd, Heale and Chartwell are open to the public all year round. All treehouse owners mentioned in this book have agreed that the reports can be written. However, as they are private, permission to visit should be sought. Interested readers can always contact the author who will put them in touch. For reasons of privacy, precise addresses are not given.

A view of the Downings' treehouse from below showing how it is firmly supported by poles

4

In Search of Treehouses

The Moat on the Hill

The road from Harleston to Halesworth winds among the low Suffolk hills. Over the horizon to the north lie Beccles and the Norfolk Broads with their images of sails gliding along in the dying evening breeze, ruined windmills silhouetted against a red sky, and bitterns booming over the reed marshes.

The Downings' instructions were clear: 'Continue past Chediston to the silage towers and turn up the steep lane opposite, to the "House on the Hill".' The lane was steeper, narrower and muddier than I had expected, but the oddest feature about the farmhouse at the top was the discovery that it was surrounded by a moat. Even moated castles are not as common these days as they used to be, but moated hilltop farmhouses, even if they do date from the sixteenth century, must be very rare indeed. This moat was no mere ditch; it was wide enough to row the Boat Race on, except for the steep bends. When I arrived, there was only a solitary red-combed Muscovy duck in residence.

The moat circled the farmhouse at a distance. In between there were sweeping lawns, outbuildings and the farmyard itself. Where the moat circumnavigated the farmyard, it split into two branches round a small, steep-wooded island. And perched high among the trees, connected by two slender suspension bridges to each side of the moat, was the treehouse.

At first glance, John and Leslie Downing did not seem the sort of people given to wasting their time and money on follies. John farms 8,000 pigs, and each day Leslie cycles into

Halesworth where she is a nurse in a doctor's surgery. But John Downing – despite the appalling handicap of a retina failure which has left him almost blind – is an innovator. When faced with the problem of how to dispose of the muck and slurry from his pig-sties, he devised a way of turning it into gas and using this to run an electricity generator. He even found a use for the waste that was left over by converting it back into fresh pig-food pellets. It was only later, when I toured the farm, that I realized the extent of the operation. This was no bucket-and-spade scheme. The pig slurry alone was enough to fill three tanker trucks each day. A sizeable gasometer stored the gas, and the several thousand watts of power needed to maintain the correct temperature for the different groups of pigs, breeders, weaners etc required a controlroom that was more like an Electricity Board power plant than a farm office.

When the Prince of Wales came down to inaugurate the scheme, he never knew he was also inaugurating the moat and, by a roundabout route, the treehouse too. The moment he left, John Downing reappraised the giant excavators he had hired which were still on site tidying things up, and directed their drivers up the lane to the House on the Hill.

'Remains of an earlier moat already existed,' he explained. 'We merely widened it.'

'We left the island,' Leslie added, as we walked across towards it, 'because we liked the clump of trees there. So instead we excavated around it.'

And there it was, as pretty a wooded island on a river as any *Swallows and Amazons* reader might care to come upon. Especially since it was capped by a treetop summerhouse.

My next surprise was to learn that the suspension bridges came first and that the treehouse was built as a means of anchoring the two suspension bridges together.

'But why a suspension bridge?' I asked incredulously, for surely a few old planks would have done just as well. John Downing pointed to the tall bank on the far side of the moat.

'It's the spill from excavating the moat. I wanted a tall bank to shelter the house. I decided to suspend the bridge between that and the treehouse. I had all these lengths of hardwood from building the piggery that needed using up.' He grinned. 'And I've always wanted to build a suspension bridge.'

It was like stepping onto one of those rope bridges that sway

Moat   Dyke

A section of the suspension bridge. The bridge came first, the treehouse was an afterthought

over crevasses in the Himalayas. There were rope supports to hold onto and slats to step on but the bridge itself dipped like a trampoline at every movement, and between the slats the moat gleamed in the evening sunlight twenty feet below. It was not exactly a bottomless pit, but I did not fancy pitching into it.

We walked across in single file, but the closer we got to the treehouse on the other side, the steeper the slats sloped, until we were climbing vertically, hauling ourselves up, hand over hand, and finally reached the treehouse verandah.

The treehouse was every bit as ingenious as the suspension bridge, and fortunately it did not sway. At a glance one could appreciate how well it was made. There was a verandah on three sides, while the house itself had big double-glazed picture windows providing marvellous views over the rolling Suffolk countryside spreading away on all sides.

The walls were insulated; the inside was lined with rough-sawn pine, washed in birch-coloured preservative; the outside

The Downings' treehouse has lovely views north over the Suffolk countryside to the river Waveney. A fine venue for skating parties on the frozen moat in winter and for a glass of wine on warm summer evenings

was painted in dark-oak stain. At one corner stood a pyramidal tower, tiled with cedar shingles. The furnishings were comfortable – a deep sofa, a stove and even a built-in stereo for music, tapes and radio.

'We love coming up here on summer evenings,' said Leslie, 'and in the winter too, when the moat freezes over and we can skate on it. We invite friends, bring some wine up here and have a party.'

At least I had remembered to bring the wine, and very enjoyable it was too, sitting up in the 'eyrie' as twilight settled over the landscape and the moon came out, shining through the treetops and silvering the moat.

Perhaps one of the most satisfying thoughts about my visit was the knowledge that the art of making and enjoying treehouses was not dying after all, especially since the treehouse itself was built of the latest materials and in the most modern fashion.

It is always difficult to appreciate how anyone can overcome their disabilities – how, for instance, Beethoven, while totally deaf, composed his symphonic masterpieces, and blind Milton wrote *Paradise Lost*, or a man like John Downing, unable to see anything unless he holds it up to the corner of his eye, could conceive, design and create something which provides such a pleasing visual effect. The combination of man-made moat, artificial island and suspension bridges serves to highlight the treehouse until it assumes the role of a distant temple in one of 'Capability' Brown's famous vistas. It is in the best tradition of Lutyens' contrived gardenscapes. Surely even Tribolo, who created Castello and its famous treehouse for the Medici dukes, would not have been disappointed.

John Downing is not running out of ideas.

'The next thing I want to do is build a drawbridge,' he insisted.

'But I'll have to be the one who gets out to lower and raise it,' objected Leslie, who does the driving.

John smiled. 'Not at all. I've been working out a photo-electric device that will do it automatically – just like those modern garage doors that you can open without getting out of the car. And after the drawbridge is completed, then . . .'

Leslie did not let him finish. She clapped her hand over his mouth, but I fancy I heard, like a strangled whisper, the words 'hanging gardens . . .' – of Halesworth, not Babylon, one presumes.

Rolleston-on-Dove

The River Dove starts life in the Peak District above Ashbourne. By the time it reaches Rolleston, it is a muddy, meandering stream, its earlier force spent, ready to join the flow of the broad River Trent a few miles away, just north of Burton.

The main road from Burton-on-Trent to Tutbury bypasses it. As a result, although Rolleston has grown, much of it is exactly as it was when Josephine Shercliff grew up there before the First World War.

Josephine Shercliff – Josie, as she liked to be called – followed an unusual profession for a woman. Forty years ago she was a war correspondent. She landed with the troops on D-Day and followed the Allied advance into Germany. Previously she had worked in Paris as a correspondent to the London *Daily Herald*, and she also reported for the *Evening Standard* and the *Daily Express*. She had entered journalism after graduating from Oxford, but her love of writing predated university by many years. It all began shortly before the First World War, when her father built her a house in one of the great oak trees that dotted their rambling garden at Rolleston-on-Dove. She recorded the event in her meticulously kept diary:

> One day I came home from boarding school to find that Father had built me a little hut in the fork of one of the giant oaks which gave our home its name. It commanded from its four windows a large stretch of the garden paddock and house and made an excellent lookout for the arrival and departure of visitors . . . The steep ladder leading to my airy hideout prevented intrusion from even the hardiest family visitors. An elaborate spiral stairway – part of an old debt to Father paid in scrap-iron – proved to be a barrier against most intruders. I was relatively safe.
>
> I spent most of my school holidays entirely in the hut only creeping into the house for an early morning shower and breakfast. I slept there on a roll-up canvas bed and cooked or warmed up meals over a perilous oil stove. I was supposed to be studying but in fact I was reading, writing, dreaming and turning a deaf ear to all cries from the house for me to come for dull meat and vegetables. I loathed Jessie's great joints of meat, and usually

Josie's treehouse became a local landmark and the subject of this village postcard. The spiral staircase had been accepted in lieu of the payment of a debt. Josie's father found a very practical use for it.

took the precaution of stealing enough provisions to last me the day. Our splendid cook daily tipped me off when something I particularly liked was on the menu.

From an early age I had been privileged to listen to poetry and prose read by my father . . . By the age of six I was already writing lyrics in a hymnlike rhythm, and by eleven I was pouring out screeds of longer poems. In the skyey freedom of the hut I became more and more prolific. Some of these passionate outpourings survive. Now they evoke nostalgia for vanished happiness in my Oak Tree hut.

A generation later her niece returned to Derbyshire and enjoyed the same treehouse. Now living at Wookey Hole, Mrs Bettina Stapleton still remembers it with great affection. As she explained to me, 'My grandfather was a wonderful person, always so cheerful and practical as well. The spiral staircase was the most unusual feature of the treehouse. In fact, the treehouse became quite a local landmark. It was even shown on early black-and-white postcards of Rolleston-on-Dove.' Bettina Stapleton also vividly recalls the bookshelves: 'The walls were lined with bookshelves from top to bottom, and there was a table that let down in front of the window.' She paused. 'The last time I ever saw it was in 1936. But it was still there after the war, until they sold the land for building.'

For fifty years or more the treehouse remained in that great oak. Not long before she died, Josie Shercliff paid a final visit to Rolleston. Perhaps it would have been better had she not done so. In one of the last entries she recorded in her diaries, she notes: 'Alas the great oak tree has vanished and with it my hut. Oak Cottage is inhabited by strangers and the orchard is buried under a rash of bungalows . . .'

Wood Butcher's Art
I had heard rumours about it for a long time. There was reputed to be a giant living in a three-storey treehouse in a wood near Canterbury with a grand piano in the top. The difficulty was in finding it.

In East Kent, Barham is more closely associated with crematoriums than treehouses. Barham church has a marvellous green copper spire, and the village street wriggles between skew-whiff timber-and-thatch houses. There is a green, a post office-cum-grocer's, a pub and a steep hill on the far side. At the top of the hill in a thirty-acre wood lives Ralph

In Search of Treehouses

The flag flies on Ralph Curry's treehouse near Canterbury. The treehouse was built in ten days by Ralph and his friends Reg Caile, a tree surgeon and Steve Beldham, a local blacksmith. Once the piano was lofted above, the celebratory party began

Curry, not exactly a giant from Jack and the Beanstalk but an impressive enough figure nevertheless. With his flaming red beard, corduroys and boots he might have strode out of the Canadian Rockies, axe in hand.

By profession Ralph is a tree surgeon, and a more knowledgeable and dedicated treeman would be hard to find. His woodland glade is dotted with rare species of trees from all over the world.

Tucked to one side of the glade, supported by two oak trees and partly by telegraph poles, stands the treehouse. Like everything Ralph does, it is massively built. To make doors he peels off slabs of oak from a felled tree trunk with a chainsaw a yard long. Everything else, walls, floors and furniture, seems to be sawn-down telegraph poles. One has the impression that these are the smallest units Ralph is prepared to work in. He does not call it carpentry, but wood butchery, and as far as he is concerned, his treehouse is a fine example of the wood butcher's art.

Wood butchers and DIY enthusiasts are a world apart. Neatly sized aluminium window frames and Black & Decker tool kits do not apply to the wood butcher's art. No wood butcher worth the name would invest in a screwdriver. Ralph Curry's massive doors are supported on equally massive hinges personally forged by a willing blacksmith. The six-inch screws used to keep them in place are smashed home with a sledgehammer.

In fact, the rumoured three storeys are only two, and the grand piano turns out to be an upright, but Ralph cannot be held to blame when myth and legend take over from reality. The piano gets its fair share of use, for Ralph is also a jazz musician and can easily swap the piano for the trumpet or his favourite instrument, the saxophone. Because the treehouse has a tendency to sway, the gramophone is suspended by ropes from the ceiling, so that the needle does not jump each time the wind blows or guests clump up the stairway outside.

Ralph has adapted the treehouse to provide maximum comfort. The corrugated iron roof is lined with felt, and there is a large woodburning stove complete with an oven for his Sunday roasts. A calor-gas stove in the corner brews up the ever-ready cup of coffee. A five-litre bottle of Johnny Walker occupies pride of place on the table. Ralph is famous for dispensing hospitality. The most notable examples are his Sunday breakfasts. Except during monsoon conditions, a huge fire is blazing in the glade below the treehouse and in the biggest frying-pan imaginable bacon, eggs and mushrooms sizzle. Pulled out from under the treehouse is a scattering of tatty armchairs, and here a most heterogeneous collection of friends and acquaintances gather once they have played the obligatory game of tennis on Barham village's one and only court – philosophers from the University of Kent, tax inspectors from Maidstone, musicians from the Hamburg Symphony Orchestra, jazz trumpeters from Canterbury, an undertaker, a sculptress from Broadstairs, a palm-reader from Folkestone: the list is endless. The only profession not represented in the glade on a Sunday morning seems to be planning officers. These and treehouse-dwellers do not necessarily see eye to eye, and Ralph is currently concerned by the fact that his local PO has acquired a microlight aircraft. He is worried in case he will be spotted when the autumn leaves fall.

The law does not have a great deal to say about treehouses.

The generally held opinion is that, if a structure is small and not permanent, it does not need permission. But treehouse enthusiasts would rather not put that to the test.

As to his treehouse's construction, Ralph Curry maintains: 'The best way to fix a treehouse in position is to use bolts,' he insists. 'This allows the tree to go on growing.' And to allow trees to go on growing is a very important factor in his work as a tree surgeon. He hates topping trees. 'Chopping their heads off', he calls it, and considers topping little different from pronouncing a death sentence. Far more preferable in his opinion is to high prune so that a view can be obtained through the trees and not over a 'hedge'.

Come the spring and he'll be off again on another of his expeditions to remote and far-away places. He is particularly attracted to the far north of Canada, exploring the headwaters

Ralph built this mini version for the younger generation, Alexi, Oliver and Clio

of the Mackenzie River and the Great Slave Lake by canoe. Unlike many of us, for him isolation holds no perils. He has just returned from a winter opal-mining in Australia.

The Enchanted Treehouse
The first time I walked into that wood, near Chilham, in Kent, there was bracken waist deep, and the leaves were yellowing; season of toadstools and woodsmoke and the autumnal whiff of decay. Six months passed, taking away with it winter, snow and damp, bare twigs in a frosty sky, animal tracks in the snow. Now, as I tried to remember the way back, it was early May – warm spring sunshine, carpets of bluebells, buds bursting into sudden puffs of green leaves.

The treehouse was the sort of place one had to return to, one of those scenes imprinted years back in the infancy of memory, the picture-book instincts we are born with, and as with all things beautiful there was a measure of sadness too, a sense of loss and abandonment. Plastic sheeting had been pulled down over the glass windows like dustsheets over the furniture of empty houses, and to make matters worse, vandals had been through it, sacking it as the Goths sacked Rome, with indiscriminate and callous recklessness. Yet for all this, it still possessed enchantment. For a start, it was so unexpected. Like a fairytale castle, it suddenly appeared between the trees. You could walk just a few yards away and never discover it, never look up and see it spread out between three oak trees, almost as if it were tethered on thin air. And as you climbed up the winding, half-rotted staircase, you could feel you were entering somewhere magic, the sort of place where a sleeping princess had lain under a spell for a thousand years.

The wood itself was a splendid place – mighty old beech trees with straight grey boles towering into the sky, dark, secretive yews, a stray ash struggling for light, sweet chestnuts splayed with bulky leaves, even a Scots pine or two, their bare red-barked limbs hoisted aloft for squirrels to leap from. And here and there a sudden change – a thicket of silver birches, a mysterious grove of oaks.

Ralph led me in. He had come upon the treehouse while doing some forest replanting. The place intrigued him. It was still and silent. If birds sang, we never heard them. When I questioned him, he knew little more than I did. A doctor from London had owned the woods. Now he had gone overseas.

The lower floor of the treehouse in Chilham Woods is now protected by wraparound plastic

His wife had become interested in the mystical; Buddhism and paganism mixed together. The treehouse had been built for her by an Australian shepherd, or maybe a bush pilot. No one knew for sure, or cared. All the actors had long since departed, the husband, the wife, the builder. Only the treehouse remained.

The treehouse was perched upon a great triangular platform that stretched between the three oaks. Like the handmade houses of California, the treehouse had grown and grown. Windows that started square became triangular,

A view of the stairway and terrace from below, Chilham Woods

ovals, circles. The walls vanished under the sweeping eaves of a curved wing of roof, like a Le Corbusier church, and above it, spindly and twisted as a witch's hat, a strange shingled spire that at once reminded me of the pyramidal spire of the treehouse at Halesworth and the pointed cap of the church in the tree in Normandy. Was it some secret treehouse hallmark – like a Masonic handshake, this twisted spire? The treehouse itself was on two levels, a large empty communal room with bench seats built into the walls, and a ladder leading up into a loft, with sloping windows cut into the sloping roof. It was big, at least fifteen feet in diameter, but for what it had been used there was no evidence at all. It could have held a witches' coven, or splendid parties, or just a place to come to alone and meditate.

How long it would last was open to question, for although the house itself was built of hardwood, the platform, the railings and the stairway were not. For the most part they were already semi-rotted and we walked across gingerly, clutching at branches for safety in case the platform collapsed under us. The staircase was a most ingenious construction, spiralling around one of the oak-tree supports.

Perhaps it would be possible to trace the owners, to find out why it was built and why it was abandoned. Yet in a way that seemed an intrusion. The treehouse was like a blank page of history that each new explorer would write about as he wished. Unless the treehouse is reclaimed and renovated, it will not be many seasons before it vanishes altogether. In fact, as we picked our way carefully through the bluebells, when I glanced back I could not even see it. The wood had already swallowed it up as if it had never been.

Suburban Treehouses

In Fort Road, Gosport, in a bungalow garden overlooking the Solent and the Isle of Wight beyond, stands a treehouse. The owner of the bungalow is a carpenter by profession, and the treehouse is therefore very well built. It is propped up by three trees, with a trellised verandah on two sides. Making the most of the space available under the treehouse platform, there is room for a caravan and a log pile.

The treehouse was originally built as a den for the carpenter's teenage son. The owner happens to be a keen model railway enthusiast, and the caravan below houses his hobby, while the son in the treehouse upstairs has outgrown such childish pursuits! The rest of the garden is inhabited by Snow White and the Seven Dwarfs: merry gnomes grin from every corner of the shrubbery.

I suspect that treehouses have been a popular enchantment with children long before J. M. Barrie immortalized them: 'I shall live with Tink,' said he [Peter Pan], 'in the little house we built for Wendy. The fairies are fixing it high up beside their nests in the treetops . . .' But when landscape gardener Jay Boyce's two sons, Christopher and James, begged him to build them a treehouse in the garden of their home at Vicarage Lane, King's Langley, they got more than their wildest dreams, for Jay built them an ark.

'It was made out of some packing cases when we came back from Australia, and battens from the roof of our house when it was re-inforced.' Jay was part-time teaching at the Rudolph Steiner school, and he constructed the treehouse during the summer holidays. He built it up in boughs of an old apple tree,

Fort Road treehouse, Gosport. Treehouses are very adaptable to urban life

a Blenheim Orange. Inside, there was space for two bunk beds. A skylight in the roof gave all the light needed. Once the boys had climbed the rope ladder and clambered in through the door at the end, they could haul the ladder up, after them. Snug inside their ark, floating high among the branches, they could dream to their hearts content, raising their Jolly Roger and buccaneering the storm-tossed seas outside.

The Smallest Treehouse in the World

Dark, lowering clouds mustered threateningly over the bleak northern moors the afternoon I set out to look for a treehouse that stood in a 'great tree' up on the fell country of North Yorkshire. Stone walls and clumps of sheltering trees clung to the bare hillsides.

This was not natural treehouse country by any means but

the editor of the *Stockport and Darlington Times* had sent me a cutting from his paper's 'Spectators Notes', and journalists never lie.

The press clipping read as follows: 'My curiosity was aroused the other day by a sturdy hut in a great tree on the Kirby Sigston to Borrowby Road, near a nice house in mellowed stone that looks as if it has strayed out of the Cotswolds. The hut had the air of having been a hideaway for generations of children.'

I had been re-reading *Swiss Family Robinson*. As I drove across the bleak windswept moors, blasted from time to time by black rain squalls, my imagination had re-created the sturdy little hut. There were rope ladders, a verandah, a thatched roof with overhanging eaves, perhaps even a hammock or two.

In the gathering dusk the straggling houses of Borrowby fell away. As I climbed up a narrow lane, the clouds lifted just a fraction to the far west, and the setting sun gleamed over the high moors. A mile ahead a great tree stood silhouetted on the bare slope. I drove faster, craning my neck for a better view. For a moment I refused to believe my eyes, but there was no doubting what I saw. Set in the lower branches of this tall hedgerow tree, highlighted by the golden sunset, was a treehouse no bigger than a very large box with a hole in the bottom – hardly big enough even for a pigmy to squeeze inside. All those grand dimensions I had created in my mind fled, leaving me alone on the moors in the twilight gazing at this hide-away hut in the great tree on the Kirby Sigston road. I glanced down at the *Spectator* notes I was clutching, to see if by any chance I could have been in error, but half a mile down a farm track to the west stood 'the house in mellowed stone', and with reluctance I had to agree there was no mistake. Why should there be? After all, journalists never lie.

Hillaby's Hide

A children's treehouse that once provided refuge for a famous explorer stood in a lime tree in Church Stretton. In his book *Journey through England,* John Hillaby – who was equally at ease taking a camel across the bandit-infested north-eastern deserts of Kenya to explore the Jade Sea – describes how he spent the night in Church Stretton.

Church Stretton lies astride the old Roman Watling Street

'The smallest treehouse in the world . . . in a great tree on the Kirby Sigston–Borrowby Road,' declared the Stockport and Darlington Times

from Hereford to Shrewsbury. On the west the town marches bravely up into the lower slopes of the Mynd; on the east it climbs more elegantly over low hills towards Coalbrookdale. Here the town sign lies buried in cow parsley, and the spacious detached properties possess names from a forester's handbook – The Mount, The Spinney, Spring Bank, Hazelwood, The Sycamores, Larchwood, The Oaks. Every back garden along the lime-treed avenue could have played host to John Hillaby, but although I looked hard and long (as long as one can without appearing suspicious), I could discover nothing bigger than nesting boxes for tits. John Hillaby must have struck a luckier moment in Church Stretton treehouse history.

Church Stretton is a very respectable-looking place. There are no vacant lots. Long tree-lined streets of aloof, detached properties, each with their own high-hedged gardens, stretch out into the country for a greater distance than I cared to walk. On impulse I settled for a little hut built in the fork of a tree for someone's child.

It partly overhung a dark and deserted street. I climbed up, put the fly-sheet over an awkward hole in the roof and settled down among a doll's tea service and a plastic machine gun. Late at night before I slipped off to sleep, the door of the house opposite opened and, to my consternation, two women came out with a yapping poodle.

They were joined by someone else's dog. The women gossiped. I caught snatches of trivial conversation. The dogs scratched, sniffed and cocked their legs up on what supported me. Here I thought is another situation I shall have some difficulty in talking my way out of, the more since I daren't dress for fear of making a noise.

But nobody looked up. Not even the silly dogs. Only the blackbirds called chick chick angrily, incessantly, at the person who had invaded their home ground. The women went home. Doors slammed. Lights went out and Church Stretton slept.

I awoke under what seemed to be a gigantic udder. Above me, only a few inches from my nose, the fly-sheet sagged, heavy with rain. I dressed hastily before sending an impressive waterfall whooshing down into the daffodils below. At that dead-quiet hour it sounded tremendous.

Hollow Trees

> Give me again my hollow tree
> A crust of bread and liberty.
> Pope, Satire VI. Book 11

In 1647 the Wiltshire Quarter Sessions were told that John Bevin and his wife, of Brokenborough near Malmesbury, for want of a house were constrained to dwell in a hollow tree in the street 'to the great hazard of their lives. They being ancient people.'

In the same century, a cobbler of Worlingham had set up his business in a hollow oak on the common near Beccles.

Hollow oak trees, like haunted houses, are peculiarly English. In ancient times the oak was sacred to the god of thunder, because these trees are said to be more likely to be struck by lightning than any other. The druids certainly held the oak tree in great veneration. The strength, hardiness and durability of the tree have given it a special significance to the English. It is regarded as 'the King of the Forest'.

> I sit beneath your leaves, old oak,
> You mighty one of all the trees
> Within whose hollow trunk a man
> Could stable his big horse with ease.
> W. H. Davies, 'The Old Oak Tree'

Royal Oaks

A great deal of English history takes place in oak trees. Owen Glendower's Oak by the River Severn at Shelton near Shrewsbury has a girth of forty-four feet, and eight people can stand together in its hollow trunk. It is a very ancient tree, for it was in full growth on 21 July 1403 when Owen Glendower, the last independent Prince of Wales, stood in the hollow entrance and watched with dismay the final moments of the Battle of Shrewsbury, as Henry IV overcame his rebellion and killed the leader of the insurgents, Sir Henry Percy ('Hotspur').

The most famous oak tree of all can surely be none other than Boscobel's Royal Oak in which King Charles II hid after the Battle of Worcester. Arthur Bryant's *Charles II* recounts:

Hollow treehouses at the Happy Eater of Hogs Back, Surrey

'At the edge of the copse overlooking the highway was an old hollow oak. Into this at Colonel Careless's suggestion they climbed. The road below was soon busy with passers-by, and through the veil of leaves that concealed them, they could see a party of soldiers searching the woods.'

Blount's account 'The True Narrative 1660' is more elaborate: '... by the help of William Pendrill's ladder they got up into the boughs and branches of the tree which was very thick and well-spread, full of leaves so that it was impossible for anyone to discern through them. When they were both up William gave them two pillows to lie upon between the thickest of the branches, and the King being overwearied with travel and his sore journey began to be very sleepy....'

The Reverend G. Plaxton, Rector of Donnington between 1690 and 1703, records: 'The Royal Oak was a fair spreading tree, the boughs of it all lined and covered with ivy. Here in the thick of these boughs, the King sat in the daytime with Colonel Carlos. So that they are strangely mistaken who judge it an old hollow oak. Whereas it was a gay and flourishing tree. The "poor" remains of this Royal Oak are now fenced in by a handsome brick wall at the charge of Basil Fitzherbert Esquire.'

The reason for the term 'poor remains' is explained by Dr Stukeley, who visited Boscobel sixty-two years after the Battle of Worcester. He wrote: 'The tree was almost cut away by travellers whose curiosity led them to see it. Close side by side grows a thriving young tree from one of its acorns.'

Souvenir-hunting is nothing new! According to diarist John Evelyn in his book *Silva*: 'People never left hacking the boughs and bark of the tree till they killed it ...' Several descendants of the Royal Oak exist both in Britain and the USA. One at Dropmore in Buckinghamshire, formerly the residence of Lady Grenville, has a plaque: 'This tree raised from an acorn of the oak which sheltered Charles II at Boscobel is planted and cherished here as a memorial, not of his preservation but of the re-establishment of the Ancient and Free Monarchy of England. The true source of her prosperity and glory.' Stout words indeed.

The Bishop of Lichfield planted a seedling from the Royal Oak (or the son of the Royal Oak) as a memorial of the Diamond Jubilee of Queen Victoria in 1897. There are probably as many unrecorded offsprings of the Royal Oak as there are of King Charles himself. His birthday, 29 May, is commemorated by members of the Order of the Sealed Knot and Chelsea Pensioners who wear a sprig of oak leaves on that day.

It is interesting to reflect that Charles II's great-nephew 'Bonnie Prince Charlie', experienced a similar narrow escape nearly a hundred years later, and although he did not hide up a tree, he was certainly sheltered by one. The story of this escapade is linked with that of his staunchest ally, Ewen 'Cluny' Macpherson.

The Macpherson clan have always been staunch Catholics. Andrew Macpherson of Cluny joined the Catholic Earls supporting Mary Queen of Scots, against the English Government in the reign of Elizabeth I. His successor, Donald of Cluny, was an equally staunch supporter of Charles I, and his grandson Donald joined the uprising for the Stuart Pretender in the abortive 1715 rebellion.

When Bonnie Prince Charlie set foot in Scotland in 1745 and raised his standard at Glenfinan, one of the first clans to swear allegiance to him were the Macphersons. Their leader, Ewen 'Cluny' Macpherson, already an officer in the English Army, resigned his commission and raised 600 men from his clan to fight for Prince Charles. In fact, had the impetuous Prince listened to the advice of Lord George Murray and not taken the field at Culloden until 'Cluny's' army had arrived, things might have gone very differently.

Prince Charles was generous even in defeat and he did not hold Cluny's late arrival on the battlefield against him. They finally met on the slopes of Ben Alder, where Prince Charles sheltered for a while in 'Cluny's Cage', a secret treehouse hide-out. Cluny, 'a leader greatly beloved by his clan', would have knelt but the Prince prevented him, kissing him and saying, 'I am sorry, Cluny, you and your regiment were not at Culloden. I did not hear till very late that you was so near to have come up with us that day.'

Also sheltering with the Prince in Cluny's Cage were members of his personal retinue, Lochiel, Lochigarry, Dr Cameron, (Lochiel's brother), Macpherson of Breakachie and four of Cluny's servants, James Macpherson, his piper, Paul Macpherson, his horse-keeper, Murdoch Macpherson (whom the Prince called Murik and who like Paul could speak no English), Duncan Macpherson and Cluny's younger brother

Donald. Prince Charlie remained hidden in Cluny's treehouse cage until he was finally guided by Cluny himself to a French ship that took him 'across the water' to exile in France.

Before he left, the Prince entrusted to Cluny's charge the famous Loch Arkaig treasure, which Cluny disbursed from time to time to aid distressed Highlanders. Charles had asked him to remain in Scotland instead of following him into exile with the other Jacobite leaders, as he was 'the only person in whom he could repose the greatest confidence'.

When it became known that Cluny had sheltered Prince Charlie and aided his escape, the vindictive English Government put a £1,000 price on his head. This was an enormous sum in those days, but for all the destitution and poverty the Highlanders suffered, no one gave him away. For a further nine years he remained in hiding on his estates, almost exclusively at 'Cluny's Cage'. Eventually, in 1754, the Prince sent orders for Cluny to come to France, where he died in exile at Dunkirk on 31 January 1764.

Perhaps the greatest compliment to him was the letter the Prince wrote to him, while aboard the French ship in 1746, before it sailed:

> Macpherson of Clunie. As we are sensible of your clan's fidelity and integrity to us during our adventures in Scotland and England in the year 1745 and 1746, in recovering our just rights from the Elector of Hanover, by which you have sustained very great losses, both in your interest and person I therefore promise when it shall please God to put it in my power to make a grateful return suitable to your sufferings.
> Diralagich in Glencamyier of Locharkag, 8th Sept 1746.
> Charles, P.R.

For a description of Cluny's Cage, erstwhile royal hideaway, we turn to Robert Louis Stevenson, and Chapter 23 of his classic *Kidnapped*.

> We came at last to the foot of an exceeding steep wood, which scrambled up a craggy hillside, and was crowned by a naked precipice.
> 'It's here,' said one of the guides, and we struck up hill.
> The trees clung upon the slope, like sailors on the shrouds of a ship; and their trunks were like the rounds of a ladder, by which we mounted.

Quite at the top, and just before the rocky face of the cliff sprang above the foliage, we found that strange house which was known in the country as 'Cluny's Cage'. The trunks of several trees had been wattled across, the intervals strengthened with stakes, and the ground behind this barricade levelled up with earth to make the floor. A tree, which grew out from the hillside, was the living centre-beam of the roof. The walls were of wattle and covered with moss. The whole house had something of an egg shape; and it half hung, half stood in that steep, hillside thicket, like a wasps' nest in a green hawthorn.

Within, it was large enough to shelter five or six persons with some comfort. A projection of the cliff had been cunningly employed to be the fireplace; and the smoke rising against the face of the rock, and being not dissimilar in colour, readily escaped notice from below.

Kings (and queens) seem to have an almost obsessive association with oak trees, apart from the Royal Oak and Owen Glendower's Oak.

In Windsor Great Park stands the Conqueror's Oak in which William of Normandy sheltered.

The Reformation Oak outside Norwich marks the site of Ket's rebellion in 1549. Here 'King' Ket briefly held court, and later from the same tree the ringleaders were hanged.

The Abbot's Oak near Woburn Abbey was where the Abbot of Woburn was hanged from its branches on the direct orders of Henry VIII in 1537 during the dissolution of the monasteries.

Until recently the Parliament Oak still stood at Clipston in Sherwood Forest. Here, in 1282, Edward I hastily convened a parliament because he was hunting there with his nobles when a messenger arrived to declare that a Welsh rebellion had broken out under the leadership of Llewelyn.

From the Queen's Oak at Huntingfield in Suffolk Queen Elizabeth I shot a buck.

Ancient Oaks

Maybe the most famous oak tree is the Major Oak in Sherwood Forest, a national shrine now protected by English Heritage. According to legend, Robin Hood dwelt here with his band of outlaws, for tradition has it that this was a fully grown tree in the reign of King John. The hollow will hold fifteen people, it is claimed. The tree's girth is nearly forty feet, and the head of the tree covers a circumference of over 250 feet.

Nowadays a well-worn trail leads from the Visitors Centre through the forest. Most of the trees are giant old stagheaded oaks. The Major Oak is certainly an impressive sight. Even though many of its massive limbs are supported on props, it still appears remarkably healthy. A perimeter fence has been put up to discourage the 30,000 or so annual visitors from trampling down the earth and damaging the roots underground. Inside the actual hollow, the walls have been painted over with fungicide. Otherwise it is quite empty. But we only have to close our eyes to imagine all those many adventures of Robin Hood we grew to love and copy as children.

The Cressage Oak in Shropshire is famous because it was under this tree that St Augustine met the natives back in the sixth century, when he brought Christianity to England.

There are records of amazingly large hollow oak trees in

Robin Hood's hollow oak in Sherwood Forest.
Reputedly seventeen men could cram inside it – they must have been thin!

Hollow Trees

The famous Cowthorpe Oak, 'Long past its prime but not dead'

England, some still standing. At Meavy in Devon, there is an oak tree near the church lychgate, twenty-five feet in circumference. It dates back to Saxon times. As many as nine people are said to have dined inside at one time. But that is nothing when compared with the Cowthorpe Oak near Wetherby in Yorkshire. That tree is over 1,500 years old and 'will hold seventy people inside'. Sometimes stories of hollow oak trees sound strangely akin to fishermen's tales, as when Wallace's Oak at Elderslie near Paisley in Scotland is said to have sheltered Sir William Wallace and 300 of his men!

One famous oak tree was the Rosemaund Oak in Herefordshire. It was so highly regarded that the local Naturalists Association – the Woolhope Field Club – wrote an article about it in their magazine *The Woolhope Transactions*. In elegant Victorian prose the description begins:

THE ROSEMAUND OAK (*Quercus Pedunculata*). – The remains of this grand old tree are still growing in the Oak meadow at Rosemaund, in the parish of Felton, on the estate of Henry Pitt, Esq. It stands on high rising ground near the house, and although it is perfectly hollow and has lost all its large limbs, it has considerable vitality and an abundance of foliage. One side of the trunk is fitted with a doorway, and seats are placed round the inside. It is open to the top, and thus it is converted into a summer-house at once roomy and airy. The inside has a diameter of about 6 feet. Its circumference at 5 feet from the ground is no less than 34 feet. It is the remains of a very magnificent tree. Who can say its age or the scenes it has witnessed? Perchance it might itself say –

> 'In my great grandsires trunk did Druids dwell,
> My grandsire with the Roman Eagle fell,
> Myself a stripling when my father bore
> Victorious Edward to the Gallic shore.'

Decay is making sad havoc with it. Spaces have to be filled up here and there with boards to make the summer house habitable. Beneath its roots many rabbits have found a home. The end of its long life is approaching, though it may yet last out a few more generations of men and of rabbits.

The Rosemaund Oak in 1870. A popular picnic venue

The Yew
Apart from the oak, perhaps the tree most traditionally associated with Old England is the yew, not least because – as every schoolboy knows – its supple limbs provided longbows for the famous English archers at Agincourt.

The reason the yew tree is grown in churchyards is because it was regarded from the time of the druids as a symbol of immortality. In a way this seems rather a paradox since its leaves and berries are very poisonous, and placing yew branches over someone's porch was a sign of cursing them to death.

There are some enormous and ancient yew trees in England. John Evelyn records in his *Silva* a yew tree at Brabourne in Kent with a girth of sixty feet. In Darley churchyard in Derbyshire stands a yew with a thirty-three-foot girth claimed to be 2,000 years old. Continuing the contest to be oldest yew, there is the one at Fortingal in Perthshire, 2,000–3,000 years old. The largest yew in Wales stands in the famous grove at Mamhilad, Gwent, and is over thirty-one feet in girth. The yew in Aldworth churchyard was mentioned in Tennyson's 'In Memoriam' and has a circumference of twenty-seven feet. It looks decayed but still flourishes. At Stoke Poges stands the famous yew tree where Gray's 'Elegy' was composed.

As yew trees are rarely hollow, there is no great scope for houses inside them, but at Barfreston in Kent a little house was built up a yew tree to protect the bell, which is connected by an iron rod across to the church tower allowing the bell to be rung from inside. Nowadays only the roof and frame remain.

The Liberty Oak
In America the oak tree is the tree of liberty. 'Tie a yellow ribbon round the old oak tree' is not merely the line of a song. Whenever Americans overseas have been taken prisoner or hostage, citizens back home, including the President in the White House, make this symbolic gesture.

The tree chosen was not necessarily the oak. During the War of Independence the fast-growing poplar was planted as 'a symbol of *growing* independence'. In the early years of the French Revolution the Jacobins of Paris decorated trees with coloured ribbons to indicated liberty, equality, fraternity. Trees of Liberty were also planted by the Italians in the revolutionary war of 1848.

Church bell in a yew tree at Barfreston, near Canterbury

But to some unfortunate Frenchmen, an oak had the opposite meaning. The Honour Oak at Whitchurch near Tavistock, was the boundary limit for French prisoners on parole from Princetown Prison during the war years 1803–14.

Snow White's Lodgings

Clifford Matthews is no ordinary Isle of Wight timber merchant. His great-grandfather started the business, cutting and stripping oak-coppice poles and selling the bark to the local tanneries in Newport, or sending it by sailing ketch across the Solent to Portsmouth. The wood poles left over he had cut up into firewood, or spills to light lamps. It was his son who really started the timber yard. In 1900 he had three pigs; he sold them and bought a small timber business.

The present Clifford Matthews ventured into specialist wood-repair work when he was asked to create a gun carriage for one of the few remaining 'parish' guns that were originally made to protect the coastal villages against the Spanish Armada. After that the Hudson Bay Company asked him to help with building a replica of the *Nonesuch* – their first vessel ever to reach Hudson Bay. He also made guns and furniture for the replica of Drake's *Golden Hind*. Since then his son, Hilton, has carried on the craft.

Hilton Matthews was one of the early divers in the team to raise the *Mary Rose*. He has worked on a number of restoration projects in Britain and abroad. He was sent to the Falkland Isles to survey the wrecks before the invasion, and his photographs and descriptions proved invaluable during the subsequent recapture of the islands. His next project will take him to Lake Titicaca to supervise the rebuilding of an old paddle-ship.

For Clifford Matthews, timber and ships go hand in hand. He does not just make replicas: as Commodore of the Royal Victoria Yacht Club, he also sails them. It was while he was organizing outings in yachts for disabled people that the local newspaper reporter who came along to do a piece about him took one look at his garden and telephoned everyone in the media she could think of. Clifford Matthews became famous overnight. The *News of the World* did a story, the BBC came down and featured him on their *Today* programme, and even the Forestry Commission wrote him up in their trade paper. The reason was his treehouse, and for a while it captured the imagination of the whole country.

For a great many years a huge hollow elm tree had dominated the Matthews' garden at Whitwell, near Ventnor, but during the last war it suffered from storm damage and Mr Matthews senior had the top chopped off in case it came crashing down. However, the hollow stump refused to die. It sprouted fresh branches every year until finally elm disease put paid to it. Clifford Matthews looked at the tree, cut off the dead branches, looked at what remained and, thinking of his grandchildren, decided to turn it into a treehouse.

The hollow stump was a good twenty feet in height and by fitting in beams he converted it into a two-storey residence. He levelled the ground floor off with concrete and carpeted it. He built a flight of steps up the outside, and cut out a door to reach the upper floor. He nailed boards across the beams, covered them with linoleum, made a table, stools and sideboard, stocked the apartment with cups, saucers, plates, knives and forks, and handed it over to his grandchildren.

He chuckled as he told me, 'Once a jackdaw got trapped

down the chimney, and another time the local Council sent a formal demand about planning permission. Fortunately it was a joke!' He paused thoughtfully. 'Once or twice in the snow, the grandchildren have seen footprints smaller than their own. Might be dwarfs, I suppose, on the lookout for a change of residence...' I waited for a wink, but he was too busy gazing out of the window.

So if Snow White does not get there first, the treehouse will continue to be enjoyed by countless generations of Matthews children. I don't expect they'd mind sharing, in any case!

Lighthouses and Castles

It was the National Trust Southern Region who sent me in the direction of a whole new dimension of treehouses.

The Tally Ho pub stands back from the junction of the Finchamstead–Eversley roads, near Wokingham in Surrey. In the gardens of the pub, beside the car-park and clearly visible from the road, stands a large, knobbly, hollow elm trunk which has been fashioned into a lighthouse. The sort where you might expect to find Long John Silver leaning over the parapet with a spy-glass while his parrot squawks 'Pieces of Eight'.

Steps cut into the base lead up to a doorway, and inside stepladders rise about fifteen feet to the circular verandah at the top, which is capped by the rather rustically crafted 'light' – a sort of giant coachlantern with open sides and a low pyramidal roof. Up the trunk are small squared windows. Closer inspection reveals that the hollow tree has been brought here, a fact readily confirmed by the landlord, Mr Silver (no relation), who bought it from a firm of Wendy House and treehouse makers in Normandy near Guildford.

To add to the maritime theme, an old Spanish galleon-style ship, built in pine logs, stands moored up close by, with a gangplank leading from its high poopdeck to the lighthouse verandah. Needless to say, all this provides a great deal of fun and fantasy for the younger generation while their elders are busy imbibing within the Tally Ho bar.

Mr Silver is rather pleased with his fleet and plans to expand it. He stood proudly and as straight-backed as any admiral taking the salute while I took my photographs.

J. M. Barrie found an original use for hollow trees in *Peter Pan*. At one point in the story, when the children are living in

The lighthouse of the Tally Ho pub near Wokingham, the schooner is on the right

their underground home below a wood, and above them the redskins are squatting in their blankets guarding the children from the pirates, the only way of communicating between the two parties is by means of the hollow trees.

The Wonderful World of Wendy Land

'Somewhere . . . in the very heart of Surrey [in Normandy in fact] a few dedicated craftsmen still wield the axe and sharpen the chisel . . .' Bayliss's *Treecraft* brochure goes on to emphasize that they will satisfy the 'Personal design and completion of individual schemes for the more discerning customer'. What quirky treehouses, one wonders, may now be dotting the countryside to satisfy the whims and fantasies of their arboreal owners?

Dodging past horrific assortments of whizzing bandsaws, chains, guillotines, treetrunks and bulldozers, I finally gained the safety of the office. A notice above the bell advised me to ring. I rang. Finally a woman appeared from a pretty timber-frame cottage beside the yard.

'Hallo, young man,' she greeted me cheerfully enough. 'Now what can I do for you?'

When I told her why I was there, her expression changed. She looked worried.

'It's my son, Anthony, you really want to see, but he's out just now. He don't mind telling you – but he don't like me telling you.'

However, she did oblige by letting me have one of the Bayliss brochures. Glancing out of the window, I realized that the drawings were tiny replicas of the little cottage next door.

'Our family, Bayliss that is, has been making Wendy Houses here in Normandy since 1920,' she told me proudly.

It was the mention of Normandy that gave me a jolt. Could there be a link with the church in the hollow tree at Allouville-Bellefosse? Perhaps Bayliss was originally a family of French woodcarvers who ventured over with William the Conqueror and settled here? Perhaps all succeeding generations of Baylisses were born with a vision of the tree-church implanted in their minds? If we try hard enough, we can convince ourselves of anything!

'What gave you the idea of making treehouses?' I asked.

'That's my son, Anthony. That was his idea. He's very artistic.'

I got out my folder and showed her the church in a tree in Normandy, France. She nodded.

'You'll have to show my son,' she said. 'He'll be interested, I'm sure.'

'But can't you tell me where some of these treehouses have gone?' I pleaded. Are there lots of them?'

After a moment's indecision, she finally cautiously admitted: 'Anthony bought up all them big dead hollow elms that died of the elm disease. He made them from those. Lighthouses mostly, and a few castles. I can't remember exactly where. There was one feller. He spent thousands on one, but he won't want me telling you about it.' Silence for a moment while she thought. She announced, 'I remember now. There's one up at the "Happy Eater", up on the Hogs Back – the road back to Farnham. You'll find it. Then you can come back and speak to Anthony. He'll like to see you, I know.'

The Hogs Back has a commanding view over half of Surrey, and on its starboard flank (towards Farnham) stands the Happy Eater. There, in a garden outside, was not only the complete range of wonderful Wendyland products but a huge red boot – presumably a relic from 'The Old Woman who Lived in a Shoe' nursery rhyme.

The Giant Boot took me instantly back to my film-editing days in Hollywood. Between Hollywood and Sunset Boulevard, at a plot appropriately named 'Cross-roads of the World', a clever architect, with an eye on the fancies of Hollywood's whimsical inhabitants, had created a whole empire of toadstools and boothouses with crooked doors and windows askew, all in white stucco and Mexican tiles. The studio I worked for occupied the toecap of 'The Old Woman Who Lived in a Shoe'.

Here, outside the Happy Eater, in addition stood a pretty timberframe and plaster Wendy House cottage, a lighthouse and a castle – carved from hollow elm trunks, all standing side by glorious side along the skyline of the South Downs.

As I drove away, it struck me that England was entering the era of mass-produced treehouses, coming off Bayliss's treehouse assembly line. After he ran out of hollow elm trunks, there were always hollow oaks – bigger and better! No wonder English Heritage were busily propping up the Major Oak in Sherwood Forest. If that should ever die and be auctioned off to Bayliss, goodness know what incredible shape he would carve it into.

And this set me wondering about the elusive client who had spent thousands on his hollow treetrunk, whose plans Anthony Bayliss and his mother guarded like a state secret. What was it and why was it done? Should he ever read this, perhaps he would come out into the open and let the world know. And that goes for all other treehouse-dwellers and wood butchers. Come forward and be counted. Let the new renaissance age of the treehouse – mass-produced or otherwise – finally dawn.

Some months later I spent a weekend with friends in the Camberley area and drove over to Normandy in the hope of seeing Anthony Bayliss. That day he was out on a job at Dartmouth. I left a message saying I would return the next morning. When I arrived, I was told he had telephoned to say he was sick and not coming in. As a result he has taken on for me the characteristic of a rather elusive, mythical figure, which perhaps is appropriate for the only man in the kingdom who actually manufactures treehouses.

Le Chêne Classé. The Monument Oak with the twin chapels at Notre Dame de la Paix at Allouville, Normandy

Treehouse Adaptations

The Restaurant in the Tree

The Chinese had no more qualms about what they ate than where they ate it, and nowhere was more popular than that amid the lofty branches, where they built large platforms, furnished with every comfort – seats, tables, lanterns and not forgetting the essential spittoon. Here they enjoyed the many courses of their exotic menus. 'If it moves, eat it.' At least if they ever ran out of chopsticks it would be the work of a moment to rustle up a new pair from the shoots above their heads.

Surely nowhere does food assume more importance than in France, and nowhere there more so than Paris – the gourmet capital of the world.

The Parisians sensibly concentrate on the quality of the cooking rather than creating pleasing surroundings – often the most unassuming restaurant offers the best food. But that does not mean to imply that the Parisians are lacking in imagination – far from it. One should not forget that the famous Moulin Rouge, haven of the *Folies Bergère*, was originally one of the many windmills of Paris.

At 69 Jardin de la Mouff is a carved oak tree. It came from a restaurant called 'Au Vieux Chêne' ('At the Old Oak') situated on the right bank of the Seine. In fact, there were two 'Au Vieux Chêne' restaurants, both built from the oak baulks of a sunken warship. The oak tree was carved from the masthead and reputedly conveyed a horrible curse on the restaurant, for every seven years precisely someone was murdered in the dining-room in full view of the proprietor. At the second 'Au Vieux Chêne' the curse was less potent, and an unpleasant

An old print picturing how the Chinese used treehouses for entertaining

accident occurred only at fourteen-year intervals.

Like citizens of all other capitals, Parisians enjoy outings into the country. Only a few miles beyond the outer boulevards the countryside is thick with *châteaux* and their gardens, parks and forests. One of the more picturesque places is Plessy Robinson, eight miles west of Paris, where a century ago people went to dine in trees.

As a race the French have never been notable eccentrics. Usually nothing could be further from their minds than to interfere with the serious business of dining by mixing it with a sense of fun and open spaces. In the circumstances, it says much for the quality of Robinson's arborial restaurants that they became so popular.

The correct name of the town is Le Plessis Robinson, and right from the beginning it was a hybrid, a commune created out of a marriage of convenience – Plessis, with its respectable families, Robinson, with its taverns and dance halls, laughter and pleasure-seekers, a haunt of writers and artists. The town came to life 150 years ago when railways started to replace the stage-coach. Plessis Robinson was on the line to Sceaux, and Parisians made full use of the railways to escape from the city and enjoy the countryside. But the fame of Robinson owes much to one man, Joseph Gueusquin, a publican. Joseph had always been impressed by the adventures of Robinson Crusoe, and as he surveyed the throngs of pleasure-seekers coming off the trains he had the ingenious idea of building a treehouse restaurant.

It was a novel and attractive scheme. He chose a large chestnut tree, already more than 200 years old, in the Rue Malabry, and up among the branches he constructed three shady bowers, prettily decorated like miniature pavilions and trellised with rambling roses. It was the romantic arboreal equivalent of dining by candlelight. Perched up in their leafy bowers the customers were able to enjoy privacy. They were served with champagne and roast chicken in baskets hauled up by means of ropes and pulleys.

The first treehouse restaurant opened in 1848. It was called 'Vrai Arbre de Robinson'. Others swiftly followed. Fortunately Rue Malabry was not lacking in giant chestnut trees. At number 113 'Le Grand Arbre' was built in 1850. In fact, at the height of its fame there were more than 200 bowers in the trees of Robinson. The success of this new craze for treehouse eating was also due to the excellent cuisine and that redoubtable breed the French waiter, who would serve an eight-course meal on the limb of an enormous chestnut tree without spilling as much as a drop of soup.

The period of greatest popularity for Plessis Robinson was before and just after the Second World War, when a visit to Robinson was considered the perfect Sunday outing. According to Michelin's Paris Guide of 1956, ' ... after having themselves restored between heaven and earth, the visitors would enjoy a game of *boule* or a dance outdoors.' It is chiefly for the Sunday dancing under the trees to the accompaniment of accordion music that Robinson will be remembered, but the entertainment did not finish there. There was horse-riding, donkey carts, picnics, bands playing. Robinson was a popular venue for wedding receptions – some in the tree bowers. All the great entertainers of the day, Maurice Chevalier included,

The restaurants at Plessis Robinson opened in 1848. Treehouse restaurants were a famous feature of this Paris suburb until the early 1970s

came out to Robinson to perform, and a popular film starring Simon Signoret and Serge Reggiani was shot there.

Sadly the treehouse restaurants no longer exist, but between the modern apartment blocks along Rue Malabry the old chestnut tree – the Vrai Arbre de Robinson where Gueusquin built his bower in 1848 – still stands. Of the three bowers that were perched '*charmantes et joyeuses*' in the treetops, there remain only the platforms, the wooden balustrades and the skeleton of the stairs.

The present-day tourist guide to Plessis Robinson invites visitors to shut their eyes and imagine it all as it once was: '*Efforçons-nous, dans le silence, d'entendre les flons-flons et les tendres chansons d'antan . . .*' 'Let us try, in the silence, to hear the drum-beats of the band and the tender songs of yesteryear.'

Who knows when some entrepreneural spirit may revive the arboreal eating habit. Even a fast-food chain of treeburger restaurants may get in on the act.

A Church in a Tree

Ever since Zeus dwelled in a hollow oak at Dordona and the Lord appeared to Abraham at the sacred 'terebinth' trees at Mamre, trees have been associated with religion.

Some experts maintain that 'Terebinth' may stand for 'turpentine'. If so, of the various trees that yield turpentine (the turpentine pine of Les Landes in France, the lofty *Suncarpia Laurifolia* of Queensland, and the Bursera shrub of Mexico) the most likely biblical choice would seem to be the *Pistacia Terebinthus*, a small tree of Asia Minor and the Mediterranean. However, others declare that it was a grove of sacred oak trees referred to in Genesis XII, 6, and Judges IX, 37. What matters is that, just as God spoke to Moses from the burning bush, so He spoke to others from the sacred tree.

To this day a grove of sacred oak trees surrounds the hilltop temple to Jupiter at Cumae, and there are oaks around the sacred pool at Delphi where the Castalia spring gushes out of Mt. Parnassos. Here visitors can still drink the waters of Lethe – the waters of forgetfulness, just as supplicants to the oracle did centuries ago. At Dordona, the priestesses of Zeus interpreted his divine messages from the rustling of the leaves. The tree was his mouthpiece, and the leaves rustled in a meaningful way when Zeus was asked a question. Nymphs of the sacred oak tree were called dryads.

Willows were also holy trees – there was even a cult of willow worshippers at Phthiotis. Willow was the rain-making tree. Even today in Italy (notably in Lombardy), the branches of pollarded willows are twined into large roomy semispherical bowers in which effigies of the Virgin Mary are placed. The actual treehouse bower shape is supposed to represent her halo. This tradition was much more common in medieval times, and it could be that Shakespeare was alluding to it when, in *Twelfth Night*, Viola offers, 'Make me a willow cabin, at your gate.'

Tree worship had never died out. In northern Europe the cult was not simply peculiar to Celts and Druids. In Lithuania, oak trees were worshipped as sacred objects until the fourteenth century. In Prussia circular villages were built around sacred oak trees which were decorated with idols. The oak trees were inhabited by gods who gave responses through a special priest called 'God's mouth'. The Pino Santo (Holy Pine) on the island of Palma in the Canary Islands was an example of a venerated tree laden with sacred relics. Here the Catholic Church embraced and continued an ancient and earlier tradition.

In Sri Lanka the Bo tree (*Ficus Religiosa*) is venerated by Hindu and Buddhist alike. It was while meditating beneath a Bo tree that Buddha gained enlightenment. The Bo tree's branches are always strung with flags, and a shrine is invariably built beside or around the base of the tree. Even the buses stop while the conductor dashes out to utter a prayer and drop a coin at the shrine.

Other rites involving trees, carried on to this day in various parts of the world, include tree-burial, especially among the primitive Gond tribes of Central India and in Papua New Guinea, where the corpses are placed in trees and in treehouses. In Bengal there is also tree marriage, where an integral part of wedding ceremony is to fasten the nuptial pair by thread to the mango tree. In West Africa the Yoruba tribe believe that souls about to be born live in trees, and women often pray to the trees to send them children.

The *Nouveau Journal des Voyages* (1882) describes a dead tree in China which supports three large shrines, perched around the massive trunk, with another shrine within the hollow interior.

But possibly the only church built in a tree that still remains in daily use after 800 years is in France — a church in an oak tree at Allouville-Bellefosse in Normandy.

Allouville is reached by driving west from Rouen or east from Le Havre along the E1, and turning off the Yvetot bypass onto the Cuadebec road. After a few miles there is a large old farmhouse restaurant with red shutters, on the right side of the road. The narrow lane beside it, half hidden by tall hedgerows, crosses rolling downland where one is extremely lucky not to find the way blocked by a muddy tractor, until the sleepy crossroads village of Allouville-Bellefosse is reached. The average road map does not even mark it, so unless one is carrying a large-scale Michelin of the area, when in doubt it is

General view of Le Chêne Classé. A chapel for eight hundred years

In a Chinese village, a dead tree has been turned into a vertical holy precinct

best to ask. Locals are accustomed to anxious inquiries in halting French from foreign motorists for directions to '*le grand arbre avec l'eglise*' or '*la fameuse eglise dans le vieux chêne*'. (Try not to say '*chien*', else it sounds even odder!)

In fact, once one has reached the village, 'Le Chêne Classé' is impossible to miss, for this immense stag-headed oak has pride of place in the churchyard, beside the road. Its trunk is thickly covered with ivy, and the spreading limbs are lashed together for mutual support with a cat's cradle of steel cables.

The central bole of the tree has been dead for centuries, possibly struck by lightning. At fifty feet, the top has been covered with a stubby spire made out of shingles from the oak itself, capped by a simple bronze cross. Lower down, the stumps of former limbs have been carefully protected by little shingled roofs and walls, creating the suggestion that the tree is inhabited by elves or fairies – like one of those children's Advent calendar trees, where a new window is opened each day as Christmas approaches.

This towering oak must have been a mighty tree long before William, Duke of Normandy, set out to conquer England in 1066, for the chapels (there are two, one above the other) within its great bole have been in constant use for over 800 years before even the foundations of the present bricks-and-mortar church nearby were ever laid.

Fortunately for Allouville, whose sole claim to fame is its church within a tree, the oak is very much alive. The heavy limbs sprout flourishing masses of leaves each spring, and in winter the clinging ivy creates a reassuring evergreen effect.

As with all churches, restoration takes place from time to time, the last at Allouville being in 1932, when the present balustraded staircase was rebuilt to give access to the upper chapel.

A notice above the hollow opening into the lower chapel severely warns any would-be vandals: '*Avis il est défendu sous peine d'amende d'escalader le balustrade qui entoure le chêne, d'enlever l'ecorce et les rameaux du chêne, d'en enlever les feuilles. Procès verbal sera dressé pour les contrevenants!*' ('Be warned that it is forbidden, under pain of a fine, to remove the bark and branches of the oak or the leaves. Civil action will be taken against those who do so!')

Just above the gap in the trunk one must squeeze through to get into the lower chapel, where another sign suggests an earlier restoration:

A Notre Dame de la paix
Erigée par m'l'arbre
De détroit curé
D'Allouville en 1696.

> To Our Lady of Peace
> Erected at the tree
> In memory of the priest
> Of Allouville in 1696.

'Notre Dame' – the greatest cathedral in France, and also a humble chapel within an old hollow oak tree!

The lower chapel has space inside for several people. At the back stands an oak altar ornately decorated with statuettes of the Madonna. A bronze carving in the panelled alcove behind depicts the Virgin Mary cradling the baby Jesus. This chapel is still in regular use and remains a focal part of all traditional village celebrations and fêtes through the year. The upper chapel (the 'oratory') is reached by the wooded balustraded staircase encircling the tree. This second chapel is a little smaller. Protected by a wooden door with iron bars, the panelled walls suggest a confessional. A large carved Christ on a cross centres the far side. Below it an ancient worm-holed sign exhorts worshippers not to write anything on the walls. Rather surprising to find such a sign on the figure of Christ!

'On est instamment priéz de ne rien inscrire sur les lambris de la Sanctuaire' – 'One is earnestly requested to write nothing on the wainscoating of the sanctuary'. There is obviously nothing new about the problem of graffiti.

The origins of these twin chapels in the oak tree have been long forgotten, but it is not unlikely that the Celts may have been worshipping the very same *'chêne'* or its predecessor on the same site for centuries before the Christians adopted it. Perhaps even St Augustine stopped here on his way north to convert King Ethelbert of Kent to Christianity and become the first Archbishop of Canterbury. Later he met English leaders under the hollow Cressage Oak in Shropshire in a bid to gain their allegiance to the Catholic Church.

Many a building has survived the centuries because of the protection offered by the Church. In Rome, the present-day Pantheon where the kings of Italy were entombed was the ancient temple to Agrippa. Here in Allouville, a tiny village in the heart of rural Normandy, an ancient oak that was probably a sturdy tree even as the last legions departed from Gaul contains one of the smallest churches in the world, Notre Dame.

Directly across the road, the shop window of the village

store is crammed with every conceivable souvenir depicting the famous Chêne Classé—ashtrays, china plates of ever increasing dimensions, teaspoons, candlesticks, mugs, even cumbersome copies of the tree itself, looking rather like woody garden gnomes. On opening the shop door, a bell clangs and after a wait *la patronne* appears, rolling up her sleeves, ready to sell stamps, brooms, batteries, pots, pans and her whole range of miniatures of the 'Church in the Oak Tree'.

The chapel of Notre Dame in the hollow oak at Allouville

The Pub in a Tree

A treehouse existed until just after the last war at an old hostelry, 'The House in the Tree', in Haydens Elm between Cheltenham and Gloucester.

For many centuries the pub was actually up in the tree. I have had letters from people and spoken to regulars who can well remember being served with cider from barrels kept in 'The House in the Tree'.

How it all began may be explained by a local legend concerning a certain Walter the Archer.

Walter, it seems, was deeply in love with a girl named Maud Bowen. She often walked to the market in Cheltenham, and when she failed to return one night, Walter went off in search of her. Hearing screams from the direction of the river, he hurried up to discover Maud struggling on the bridge with her wicked uncle Geoffrey, who was trying to abduct her.

Unfortunately, Geoffrey was not the only one after Maud. The Lord of the Manor was waiting there too. Walter slotted

An early photograph of the Old House in the Tree

an arrow into his bow and shot dead the uncle, but Maud was so surprised that she fainted and fell into the stream. (It sounds like a silent movie from the twenties.) The poor girl was drowning, the Lord of the Manor was scared stiff after seeing Geoffrey shot, and Walter was wringing his hands, unable to go to the rescue for fear of being spotted as Geoffrey's murderer. When the rest of the village arrived on the spot, they discovered Maud drowned and Geoffrey dead, clutching a bit of her dress. Walter and the Lord of the Manor had disappeared.

At the inquest the Lord of the Manor in his capacity as sheriff declared that Maud had committed suicide. Quite what his verdict was on Geoffrey is not known. However, death by suicide meant that Maud was buried at the nearest crossroads (Haydens Elm) with an elm stake driven through her body. Her mother went crazy with grief, whereupon the Lord of the Manor evicted her from her cottage and she spent all her time sitting by her daughter's grave. Meanwhile the elm stake took root and grew into a young tree.

One day, as the Lord of the Manor passed by on his way to church, he ordered his servants to drag Maud's mother away. When they attempted to do so, one of them was mysteriously felled by an arrow. As no one spotted Walter, the archer, the Lord of the Manor declared that it was done by magic. He accused the old lady of being a witch and ordered that she be burned to death on the spot. He laughed merrily at her screams as the flames rose, until suddenly the invisible archer struck again, and he dropped dead.

It's a strange story, out of which no one emerges very creditably, certainly not even Walter who seems to have been more concerned with shooting people than rescuing them.

Be that as it may, there was until recently a great old elm still there at the crossroads, and evidence that Walter did indeed dwell at the House in the Tree pub can be found in this old local poem.

> My name, good Sir, is Walter Grey
> In days of yore I had some fame
> The Archer was my sportive name
> Part since by my avenging bow
> I've laid those unjust persons low.
> Secluded, and by feigned name,

> I've strove my best near to remain.
> A country inn was my abode
> That lay hard by old Gloucester Road.
> Twas there I dwelt until my last
> And only enemy was cast
> Into Eternity's abyss.

On the evening I arrived at the House in the Tree pub, several of the locals were busy quenching their thirst. Two of them, Dave Wilks and Tim Waller, told me about the old house that was still up there in the tree until the latter days of the last war. The story of the cider barrels went back another generation to the time when a Mr Hobbs was landlord.

'When we were boys,' declared Tim Waller, 'we used to climb up the old treehouse, but it was getting pretty shaky even then. Not a lot of customers were prepared to risk it, unless they was a-courting.'

'What happened to it in the end?' I asked.

They shrugged. It seemed that during the difficult years of the war the old treehouse rotted away, and the tree it was built in finally died of elm disease a few years ago.

'It was a big treehouse, mind,' Dave Wilks insisted, 'large enough to hold thirty people or more. Customers would often take their drinks up there of a summer's evening.'

And then the conversation turned to other things – how during the First World War German prisoners still in uniform had driven the brewery dray; in the Second World War an anti-aircraft battery was stationed in the next field. As the temptations of the House in the Tree pub were too great to resist, an electric bell was rigged up. The squad could now spend a merry evening in the pub in the safe knowledge that whoever remained on duty would buzz the alarm the moment an enemy raid was spotted. Of course, what their aim was after an evening drinking cider in the House in the Tree was anyone's guess.

> Drink hard cider as much as yer please
> Loose yer teeth and bow yer knees
> Sours yer guts and makes yer wheeze
> Turns yer words to stings o' bees
> Thins yer blood and kills yer fleas
> Drink hard cider as much as yer please.
>
> Old West Country verse

German prisoners-of-war at the time of the First World War delivering barrels to the House in the Tree pub

A Pub Round a Tree

A well-known London pub, The Mitre in Ely Court (1546), was originally built round a cherry tree.

For centuries there was a part of the county of Cambridgeshire in the very heart of the City of London. Ely Place was the site of the rose gardens, orchards and meadows belonging to the Bishop of Ely, whose church, St Etheldreda's still stands there. The strawberries from his garden were famous as far back as the reign of Richard III, according to Shakespeare, who in the words of Richard, then Duke of Gloucester, says:

> My Lord of Ely, when I was last in Holborn
> I saw good strawberries in your garden there;
> I do beseech you, send for some of them!

In Queen Elizabeth's reign, her Chancellor, Sir Christopher Hatton, leased part of Ely Place at a rental of a red rose, ten loads of hay and £10 per annum. It was during this period that the Mitre Tavern was built around the cherry tree, which was the boundary between the bishop's garden and the part leased to Sir Christopher. Because Ely Place was originally the Town Residence of the Bishops of Ely, it also had certain privileges which remain to this day. For instance no police sets foot within the iron gate of the porter's lodge unless specially summoned. The dispenser of law and order is the beadle. He is also the watchman and until comparatively recently he would call the hours through the night from 10 p.m. to 5 a.m.:

> 'Tis twelve o'clock.
> Look well to your lock,
> Your fire and your light,
> And so good-night.

The famous orchards and strawberry gardens of Ely Place have long since vanished under the foundations of the present

The treehouse in St John's Wood churchyard. Similar bowers exist at Kew Gardens

buildings. Only the name 'Hatton Garden' offers a clue to its history, but the Mitre Tavern still retains the trunk of the ancient cherry tree, displayed behind the bar.

London's tree oddities also include a plane tree in Chandos Street which has overgrown the street railings, carrying them with it as it grew until the old rails had to be cut off on either side and a new railing fitted below. But apart from similar examples at Kew Gardens, the capital's only treehouse open to the public stands in the churchyard at St John's Wood, Wellington Road, NW1. Here the branches of an ash tree have been trained downwards to cover a large wigwam-shaped iron frame completely. The result is a spacious treehouse with virtually impenetrable leafy walls screening out sun and rain and offering privacy for courting couples or a place for children to play.

The Shop under the Tree

The plane tree at the corner of Wood Street and Cheapside is probably the most valuable tree in London, not because there is a house in it but because it prevents any houses at all being built near it. This tree grows in the plot of land which is all that remains of the churchyard of St Peter Chepe, situated in Cheapside until it was destroyed in 1666 by the Fire of London. It is protected by the leases of the three remaining shops at the corner of Wood Street. These are the smallest buildings in the City's square mile. The reason for this is that an edict of 1687, the year they were built, declares that they must not be increased in height, or the remains of the churchyard be built on, so long as the plane tree is alive. As the tree is still very healthy, it may be some while before this prime site gets developed.

Wooderson's (shirt-makers) have for many years occupied the corner shop. In the glass panel of the door is an engraving of a plane tree with the words

>Woodersons
>Under the Tree

It was under this tree that Wordsworth heard a thrush singing and wrote his 'Reverie of Poor Susan':

> At the corner of Wood Street when daylight appears
> Hangs a thrush that sings loud, it has sung for three years.

A Tree Walk in Battersea

During the 1951 Festival of Britain, a treetop walk similar to those of Japan was erected high in the trees at the Battersea Fun Fair. There visitors could stroll between the trees looking down over the great pleasureground with its golden fountains and flowers, its illuminated arcades and pavilions. The tree walk connected small pavilions each topped by a gaily coloured roof – a witch's hat, brightly striped in blue and red.

Tree walk, Battersea Fun Fair, 1951. This very ornamental treetop tour of the Gardens was a popular feature of the Festival of Britain

The Railway Station in a Tree

Few of us have ever imagined in our wildest dreams that a tree would become a railway station, but that is precisely what happened on the Great Western line between Hereford and Shrewsbury.

A hundred and fifty years ago there were two huge old oak trees, 'Adam' and 'Eve', standing a hundred yards apart in the meadows by the River Lugg at Moreton, near Hereford. By then they were both past their prime. They had suffered from many a storm, had lost a lot of their branches and were completely hollow. During a particularly violent winter gale on 7 January 1839, 'Adam' was blown down, and lay for many years afterwards in the meadow; 'Eve' lost a great many branches but stayed upright. Of the two, Eve, perhaps predictably, was the more famous. The huge hollow space inside her had been well known for years. Twenty-one grown sheep had been counted coming out, and a group of thirteen people are said to have had a tea party inside. According to the *Transactions* of the Woolhope Naturalist Field Club of 1870, 'she' had long been the centre of much picnicking fun.

When the Shrewsbury-to-Hereford Railway was built, the line included Eve in its boundaries, and the hollow bole was quickly adopted as a residence by an economical navvy. The top was sloped off evenly from sixteen feet on one side to nine feet on the other, a thatched roof was put on, a brick chimney was built in the low opening on the south side with a chimney beside it, a door was fitted to the main opening on the east side, and so it became 'a family tenement compact and convenient'.

The line was finally opened in 1853, and the workman moved on. Because the tree was next to Moreton-on-Lugg Station, it was used for many years as a storage depot and a lamp room, big enough for at least six people to sit comfortably inside round a table. It was also a place where the porters could huddle for a smoke and a mug of tea. Even the thatch roof was repaired. The tree was still alive and putting out green twigs and leaves.

In June 1862 the railway line was leased in perpetuity to the Great Western Railway, the famous GWR. As a result the single line was upgraded and the station rebuilt. It was during this period that Eve became the official residence of the station master, and also the ticket office for Moreton-on-Lugg Station. As a mark of its new-found status it was decorated and painted with the GWR familiar green and gold colours, and the roof was re-thatched. Passengers quickly became accustomed to queueing up inside Eve to get their tickets. Once the station was rebuilt, however, the hollow oak reverted to being a lamp room and porter's lodge and remained so until 1869, when it became a stable for a donkey.

The tree was still alive many years later, but when its

The single-track line of the London and North-Western Railway and its unusual station at Moreton-on-Lugg

unusual history was written up in the *Railway Magazine* for 1902, sad to report, old Eve had finally expired. Concluding with a rather anatomical observation, the *Railway Magazine* reported: 'Even in its dry state the tree still measured 25ft. 8in. in circumference.' It continued:

> Readers of the RAILWAY MAGAZINE will agree that a railway station 'in a tree' is a veritable curiosity, yet there appears to be little doubt that a hollow oak tree was made to serve the utilitarian purpose of a railway station-building for some time. This, however, happened many years ago, but by the courtesy of Mr G. K. Mills, the Secretary of the Great Western Railway, we are enabled to present to our readers an illustration of this 'curious railway station' – a combination of the picturesque and useful, not often found in connection with the iron road. The

view in question is reproduced from a water-colour drawing that adorns the walls of Mr Mills' office at Paddington; and it represents a hollow tree at Moreton-on-Lugg, a small station about 2 miles north of Hereford on the Shrewsbury and Hereford section of the joint London and North-Western and Great Western Railway. As the illustration shows, the line was originally single and was opened to Hereford in 1853, being worked by a contractor, Mr T. Brassey, till June 30, 1862, when the railway was leased in perpetuity to the Great Western and London and North-Western Railways jointly. As soon as the joint lines took over the railway, the oak tree appears to have fallen from its high estate of station-house.

'Eve' at Moreton station, 1870. By turn a stable, a navvy's home, a station lamp room and finally a ticket office

The Yew Tree Tunnel

An unusual feature of Melbourne Hall grounds, in the Peak District, is the curious yew tree tunnel. It is said to have been planted during the reign of King Charles I. The actual tunnel is over a hundred yards long and is not simply an overgrown avenue, for there exists a record dated 1726 stating that its original framework had recently been removed because it had decayed.

Readers of school stories may remember a wartime book by Elinor M. Brent-Dyer called *The Chalet School Goes to It*. References in the book to a yew tunnel suggest that the author may have known the tree tunnel at Melbourne Hall. In the story, Beth, Gwensi and Daisy crawl along a narrow green tunnel formed by the trees until finally they emerge into a kind of cave in the yew trees. This, they decide, has been plainly cut by hand, for no trees would have ever grown into that particular shape by themselves. The chamber had a cone-shaped roof and was easily tall enough for them to stand in upright. It is reassuring to discover that so much of fiction is based on fact in the first place.

The Tree with a Road in It

Many of us are familiar with photographs of the famous giant redwood tree in the United States with a highway carved through the middle of it. It may come as a surprise to discover that a more modest version has existed for more than 200 years in the village of Kingsland, west of Leominster in the West Country.

Kingsland is justly proud of its famous landmark, and the tree with the road through it is depicted in the one and only postcard of the village.

In recent years, the road leading to Holgate Farm has bypassed the tree, and the lane has been reduced in importance to a footpath, guarded by a stout gate. Nevertheless, there it is, offering excellent protection from sun and rain alike, and judging from the Coca-cola cans and old crisp packets left there, it remains a popular rendezvous among the younger generation of the neighbourhood.

The Cobbler of Worlingham Common

A slightly less impressive adaptation of a tree, but one nevertheless just as ingenious and important in its own way, was

The Tree with a Road in It. An old postcard of Holgate Farm

created by an enterprising shoemaker in the village of Worlingham, near Beccles, who established his business in a great hollow oak tree on the common at the edge of the 'Great Road'.

He was immortalized by the painter Isaac Johnson of Woodbridge, Suffolk, who made a very fine picture of the hollow oak with the cobbler inside. The painting is dated 1785.

Although Worlingham Common as such no longer exists, Worlingham Park, owned by the Colville family, does. The park contains many fine old oak trees, while outside the lodge gates and opposite the village church an attractive wooden sign has been erected, showing the cobbler at work.

I recently received a letter from the Reverend Geoffrey Johnson, who has just retired as vicar of Worlingham. He confirms that the cobbler's tree stood at the eastern end of the parish opposite the old church school at the end of School Lane. He goes on to explain that when the wooden village sign was put up by the Women's Institute to mark the Coronation Silver Jubilee, most people thought the picture of the cobbler looked like a 'little old man sitting on the loo at the bottom of the garden'! In a more serious tone he concludes, 'The sign shows the crinkle-crankle wall of the Hall fruit garden still seen in Garden Lane, the River Waveney and the herons which we sometimes see down by the river.'

As a footnote he included an extract from Suckling's *Antiquities of the County of Suffolk*, Volume I, 1846:

> The eastern portion of the parish (Worlingham) consisted a few years ago of uncultivated heaths and commons. In this part of the village stands an ancient oak, whose trunk is almost concealed from view by a thriving hedge. This venerable tree, whose age is probably about five hundred years and which,
> 'Whylom had been the king of the field,'
> is now a hollow and almost sapless trunk. It afforded shelter for some years to a village cobbler, who pursued his occupation within its rind; and it is said that a blacksmith once shod a horse within it. The tradition may be true, for it measures twenty seven feet in circumference at a foot from the ground.

The Scissors Tree

A most unusual tree exists in the garden of a house in Dawlish in Devon. It has grown in such a way that the lower part of

The cobbler hard at work in the old oak, Worlingham. Note that the carving shows the Waveney river which runs nearby

the trunk has the appearance of a pair of scissors, complete with symmetrical handles. Although it is claimed to have grown naturally, one cannot help wondering what care some Victorian gardener may have lavished on it.

The original Treetops was designed for the Walkers in 1932 by Captain 'Ugly' Sheldrick. It was first used as an observation platform for their Outspan Hotel in Kenya's Aberdare Mountains

Treehouses Around the World

'Treetops' – A Hotel up a Tree

Lady Bettie Walker and her brothers, children of the Earl of Denbigh, spent a lot of their childhood in an enormous treehouse so constructed that they were safely out of reach of parental observation. It was memories of this and of James Barrie's immortal classic *Peter Pan* that inspired her to build 'Treetops' in Kenya's Aberdare Forest, a treehouse from which their guests at the Outspan Hotel could view the wild animals by night.

Lady Bettie's husand, Eric Sherbrooke Walker, had been Private Secretary to Lord Baden-Powell during the formative years of the Scout movement. In the First World War he had joined the Royal Flying Corps, and when he was shot down and taken prisoner, Baden-Powell posted him a pair of wire-cutters! Later, Walker became owner and proprietor of the Outspan Hotel in Kenya's Aberdare Forest. There was no doubt that the Walkers were an ideal team for a couple destined to create one of the most unusual and successful hotels in the world – up a tree.

Once the idea of Treetops was born, the next step was to find the ideal site. For this the Walkers had the good luck to be friends with Captain 'Ugly' Sheldrick, a retired Indian Cavalry Officer who owned a coffee plantation at Mweiga on the edge of the Aberdare mountains some ten miles from Nyeri and who knew of just the right place. With a wry grin he announced, 'There's a waterhole where the elephant drink on their way to trample on my coffee trees, blast them!'

Sheldrick's Dutch overseer took the Walkers through dense forest to an enchanting pool in a natural clearing of some two or three acres. It was on the lower slopes of the Aberdare Mountains at an altitude of some 7,000 feet, only a few miles south of the Equator, and was surrounded by Cape chestnut trees, a mass of beautiful mauve blossoms. On one side was a wide elephant path along which for centuries the herds had passed. The track ran right beneath a giant mugumu (wild fig) tree with its spreading branches and dark green foliage.

Sheldrick had previously erected his own observation platform elsewhere in the forest from which he and his friends could view the wild life unobserved. While it was always fascinating to watch the animals, the platform was rather primitive, and sitting for long periods of time in a cramped position was never comfortable. At that high altitude the setting sun brought with it chill and often intense cold. It did not require much encouragement from the Walkers to persuade Captain Sheldrick to build them a room and verandah up in the fig tree.

Within weeks the kindly Sheldrick had built an ingenious little two-room house in the fig tree. It had a verandah facing the pool. The floor was some thirty-five feet above the ground, higher than the surrounding trees, so that the wind blew the human scent away above the forest. A very tall chimney, sticking out high over the trees and reaching a height of sixty feet, took care of the smoke from the tiny wood stove. Water and provisions were brought on the heads of African boys and girls who were glad to earn a little extra money. (A girl once carelessly tipped over the car battery used for lighting, and some of the acid trickled down her back. After that there was great competition to be the bearer of the battery because she received an extra penny as danger money for each trip!)

The first overnight visitors were welcomed on the night of 6 November 1932. At that period the viewing of wildlife from the 'tree hotel' was restricted to nights around the full moon, but from its very beginning Treetops was popular with every visitor to Kenya.

In their book *Treetops Hotel*, the Walkers describe their early experiences: 'Treetops in those days was so tiny it had room for only two guests. Either my wife or I used to do the cooking, washing-up and bed making. Sometimes our visitors gave a hand but usually they were too engrossed in watching the animals. One gracious lady, however, as soon as dinner was over, tucked up her sleeves, stacked the plates and insisted

Treetops, 1952. Where a young lady climbed up a tree a Princess and climbed down a Queen!

on seeing the task right through while her husband, the Duke of Gloucester, sipped a whisky and soda meditatively on the verandah, watching the dim shapes of rhino scrapping together in the moonlight below.'

As Treetops expanded, the time came to employ a 'Tree Hostess' to look after people at Treetops. The qualifications were:

1. To be able to use a catapult on the baboon which sometimes snatched cakes off the tea table.
2. To be unafraid of big game.
3. To know all about forest animals.
4. To have the qualifications and charm of an air hostess.

Treetops was famous for its hospitality, but there were certain unwelcome guests:

In the early days at Treetops we did not bother to put any glass in

Treetops today. A must on every tourist's itinerary

the window of the washroom. Nobody could see in and we thought it did not matter much. Unfortunately a leopard once climbed through the window and was unable to find his way out. Since then we have fixed strong expanded metal over the washroom window. This keeps out not only the inquisitive leopard but also the baboon who used to eat the soap and get up to other mischief. One day I was taking a party of Americans to Treetops and as we approached the pool one of them exclaimed 'Gee, I didn't know we were important enough for a tickertape reception!' The trees around Treetops were gaily festooned with long strips of white paper. A baboon had climbed into the lavatory and seized a large roll of toilet paper which unwound itself as he clambered with his booty triumphantly from branch to branch.

When it was learned that Princess Elizabeth and Prince Philip would be overnight guests during their 1952 visit to Kenya, Treetops was extended to provide three bedrooms, a room for the hunter-escort, and a little dining-room with a wood-burning stove. Now for the first time floodlights were provided in the absence of the natural full moon.

During the royal holiday King George VI died in London. To quote Colonel Jim Corbett, 'A young girl climbed into a tree one day a Princess and climbed down from the tree next day – a Queen!'

Unhappily fire destroyed that first Treetops shortly after the royal visit, but it was not long before Treetops II was 'growing' on the opposite side of the waterhole. Built for the Walkers by Tom Arthur of Mweiga, it surpassed the original in so far as facilities were concerned. So great was to become its popularity that it was then three times extended to the accommodation that is seen today. The last sophistication added was central heating!

A royal visitor to the new Treetops was the Queen Mother when she visited Kenya in February 1959. As in most royal tours, unforeseen problems arose, as the Walkers relate:

> The day before she arrived at the treehouse both generators failed. Without the electric moon and the lighting and heating inside Treetops, the visit would have been a fiasco. Fortunately we found two mechanics, a Sikh and an Italian who laboured all the Monday afternoon and then sat up throughout that night coaxing the engines along.
>
> After tea, a large cow rhino suddenly emerged from the forest and started drinking at the pool almost directly under Treetops. Studying the two ugly horns sticking out of the animal's head, the Queen Mother remarked 'The last time I was in Kenya, in 1925, I saw a number of rhino from ground level and was not too fond of them. I feel much happier seeing them from this platform!'

Treetops III is perched on top of a forest of mahogany poles, intersected by stout branches of very old and large trees. The silhouetted scene is breathtaking when viewed for the first time. Just in front of the main building is an immense area of trees, the central part of which is occupied by a waterhole surrounded by a salt-lick. Buffaloes and gazelles graze undisturbed below, and footprints of elephants and rhinos are evident everywhere. Guests are warned to keep their bedroom windows closed against bothersome baboons, who without warning help themselves to handbags, wallets, sweets, clothing or whatever they can freely grab. Tea is served on the open verandah, while colobus monkeys swing on the branches nearby. Down below on the ground families of grunting warthogs mingle with grazing gazelles and antelopes.

As evening falls, Mount Kenya stands silhouetted against the sunset. The snow-covered peak towers majestically above, while down in the valley the dark shadows lengthen. Along the Equator night falls quickly, and a chill wind blows off the Aberdare Mountains. Moonrise, its light mixed with the glow from the huge spotlights which shine down on the waterhole from the Treetops rooftop, is the cue for a procession of animals making their way to the waterhole. The line is endless – hyenas, gentle little duikers, waterbucks, buffaloes, genet cats, warthogs, antelopes and the kings of them all – the elephants and rhinos; sometimes even a prowling leopard.

The modern and vastly more comfortable design of Treetops is not limited to Kenya. For the wildlife watcher, Tigertops in Nepal offers similar attractions. There are other, simpler tree lodges dotted throughout the Indian subcontinent and in South America.

An imaginary Treetops was created by R. P. Straughan in his book *Build a Jungle Zoo* (1973). His idea was to re-create a safari park in southern Florida or southern California, on a grand scale – fifty to one hundred square miles. This would include swamps and rivers and forests, together with all the animals that inhabit them. To house the visitors who would flock to enjoy this 'safari', Straughan proposed a treehouse lodge.

He describes his proposed safaris in the following words:

> A safari will consist of a dozen guests, who have the desire to spend a night in the heart of the jungle. The journey will be timed so that the party arrives at the water hole and treehouse just before dark. They will hear distant native drums, the roar of a lion and authentic noises, both natural and recorded as required to give complete authenticity to the atmosphere. Treetops, the famous jungle treehouse of Africa will be duplicated here.
>
> Erected in a huge banyan tree will be the treehouse, built high above ground for protection from prowling beasts. The house will be primitive but comfortable and will overlook the water hole, which will be the main center of attraction. Guests will be able to photograph the wild animals as they wander up to the water hole in small groups as they do in their native land. As nightfall approaches, guests may roam about the screened porch that goes completely round the house or sit in the game room which will be handsomely furnished with authentic African handicraft. The jungle sounds will lull them to sleep or keep them awake, whichever is their cup of tea.

A treehouse in New Guinea as seen by the Boy's Own Paper *in 1920*

I'm not sure what your cup of tea is, but having been on several safaris myself, varying from the lavish (where one is served chilled wine, seated around the campfire waiting for supper) to a primitive walk with the Masai (building our own thorn fences at night to keep out lions and chewing semi raw goat meat), I for one regard Mr Straughan's well-meaning plans with mixed feelings. On the other hand, perhaps it is possible to create an artificial environment more real than the real one. In addition to the taped jungle sounds, would he also plan to release swarms of mosquitoes and tsetse fly? Or is that going too far!

Hunters' Hides

A particularly functional adaptation of tree platforms is for hunting, and the British Forestry Commission even issues a booklet entitled *High Seats for Deer Management*, complete with photographs of huntsmen up on platforms peering through telescopic sights. However, this pamphlet also contains a great deal of useful information about building tree platforms:

> They must be sufficiently solid not to creak or squeak when being climbed or when the need to stretch cramped limbs becomes paramount. They must provide a safe platform from which a shot can be taken in any weather . . . The floor and the seat must also be reasonably freely draining and a tip-up seat or unattached padded plank . . . Protection from cold, cramped conditions adds considerably to the period for which a stalker can concentrate efficiently. It is worth draught-proofing the floor with old linoleum . . . If the sides are made wind-proof, as well as effectively camouflaging the stalker, they will protect him for a longer period. A Spartan disregard for cold, miserable conditions then becomes an additional asset rather than an essential attribute of a stalker!

Hides are constructed by huntsmen the world over, but possibly they are nowhere more cunningly devised than in Italy, where the walls and roofs are frequently woven from the living branches of the trees — usually an evergreen tree — and are virtually invisible even a few feet away. In the walls, at gun height, small holes are pruned out and lined with moss. Refinements include a sheet of plastic or tin tacked up inside the roof, a small open fireplace in one corner and inevitably a

Treehouses Around the World

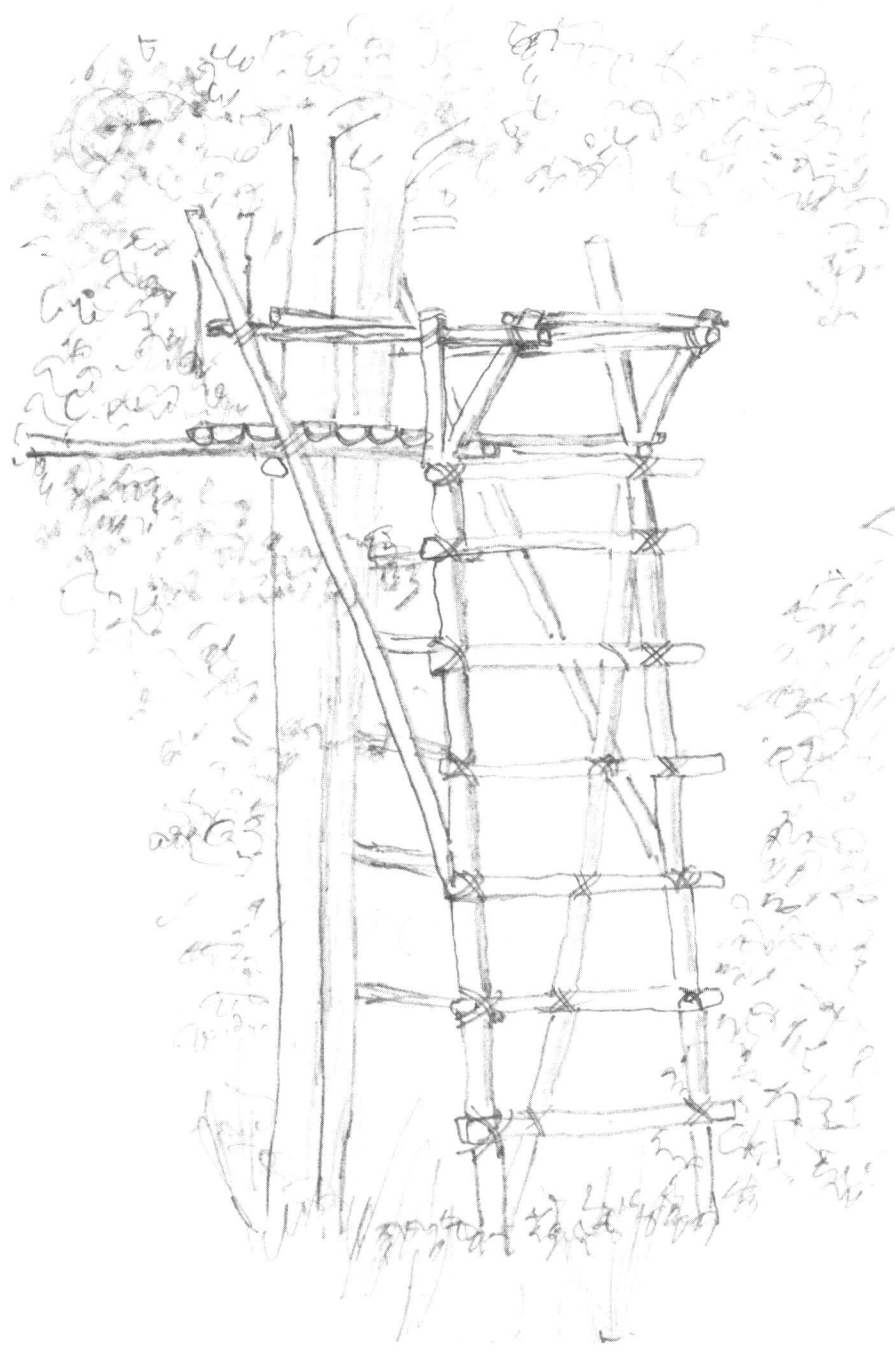

Sketch of a lean-to platform for shooting or photographing wildlife. The wire and the extra struts make it safer

bottle of grappa to provide internal heat should all else fail.

Although Big Game hunting is now frowned on and the emphasis, quite rightly, is on conserving wildlife, control and culling of game play an important part in any worthwhile conservation programme. In the Black Forest, German foresters reckon that a ratio of one deer to fifty acres is about right. A higher population density will destroy the forest regeneration and eventually cause great hardship for the deer themselves, until natural selection weeds out the poorer specimens.

Indian villages in remote areas are from time to time troubled by man-eating tigers, who, once having tasted human flesh and discovered how easy it is to capture, can cause havoc and tragedy. When trackers have identified the tiger's hunting runs, a convenient spot is selected – usually a small clearing overlooked by a tall tree in which the hunters build their shooting platforms (machans). A goat is then tied to a stake in the clearing for bait. Its bleats should attract the

A hide for culling deer in Forestry Commission woods near Canterbury

tiger, but often several nights of patient waiting pass in the uncomfortable machan – little more than a few planks propped in the branches – before the tiger appears. In the darkness or in the grey misty dawn light a critical shot is by no means easy, especially when one's limbs are cramped and stiff and one's reflexes dulled by sleeplessness. The worst danger is to wound the tiger and not kill it, since a wounded tiger is likely to take revenge on any hapless child leading a water buffalo or a peasant farmer working his field.

Nowadays the machan offers an ideal location for photographing wildlife. Silence, however, is essential, for tigers do not take kindly to having their meals disturbed. To have one growling ferociously just below one's feet can be a daunting experience.

American Hand-Made Houses

Wood butchery reaches its highest art form in the United States, where individualism is the key. Ever since Frank Lloyd Wright encouraged his students to make their own dwellings in desert scrub, using whatever materials they could lay their hands on, successive generations of would-be architects have followed this tradition.

The forests of Maine and New Hampshire are full of handmade houses, many built up trees, but nowhere do they achieve such pinnacles of bizarre creativity and ingenious design as in California.

The trick seems to be, according to experts on the subject, 'Just get a start and let it grow.' They go on: 'Consult the "old Farmers Almanac", or Second Corinthians, or the I Ching, but keep right on with it. And if the inspectors come around, call your place a "potting shed", a "summer camp", a "mining claim" – anything that pops into your head. . . . And when they keep on shoving, call it a firehouse, a briar patch, a commune – whatever riles them most. If they take to threatening you, demand a jury trial and that holds them off a while.'

California has the advantage that the coast throws up some of the largest pieces of driftwood anywhere in the world, already shaped and sculpted by the sea into a personality all of its own. Slabs for stairs, shaped bits for handrails – it is said that if you wait long enough, the Pacific Ocean throws up anything you want: Indian totem poles, four-poster bedposts, oildrums to make stoves out of, salvaged lumber, rocking

Open-plan design? Or a place for meditation? Treehouses take unusual forms in the Californian Redwood forests

chairs, windowframes, nets, jamjars, rusted hurricane lanterns, bust clocks, chipped plates, broken mirrors, old doors, fragments of stained glass, waterpipes, wire, bedpans, old windshields, ram skulls, wine bottles. And there's a use for everything, even the cow-horns. I met one man who made neat little oil lamps out of condensed milk cans.

Way up above the Suwannee River
A recent photograph in the *Independent* newspaper showed a treehouse cabin belonging to John Thurston being winched

by helicopter from its perch 40 feet above the Suwannee river after a Miami property developer, who owned the land, insisted on it being moved. Mr Thurston decided to retain his independent life style by having the treehouse lowered onto a boat. Life in the treetops to life afloat in one easy step – with the aid of a helicopter!

Treehouses in Hollywood

Perhaps some of the most famous treehouses are those seen in the early Johnny Weismuller *Tarzan* films and in the more recent attempt to portray the real story of Edgar Rice Burroughs' *Tarzan of the Apes* under the title *Lord Greystoke*.

For all these films wonderful treehouses were built in the

A handmade house in California

branches of trees on 'sets' in Florida, where the earlier films were shot, or in Hollywood studios. According to these films, treehouse life must have reached a pinnacle of comfort and sophistication. The reality of the jungle is very different!

There was one movie in which a tree was not only used to support the camera cranes but also to provide a stage for the actors. In *Quality Street* (1927), director Sidney Crane topped a big oak tree and built a camera platform over the lopped-off branches. Lower down, a circular platform was built around the tree, some ten feet above the ground, for a dance routine. The camera on the platform could be rapidly tracked round and round the tree to film the dance. Meanwhile musicians to supply the rhythm had their places below the platform.

A Treehouse in a Rain Tree

In the entire Indian subcontinent there is possibly no grander tree than the rain tree, *Pithecolobium Saman*. In moist regions it assumes a great size. In his *Tropical Planting and Gardening*, H. F. MacMillan writes: 'For scenic effect it is difficult to surpass the beauty of isolated specimen trees of well-balanced proportions with spreading branches set at wide distances....' ('Under the spreading chestnut tree', could be supplanted in the tropics by 'Under the spreading rain tree'.) The massive trunk with its rather hairy bark splits up at a low height into a symmetrical pattern of equally massive boughs sloping evenly outwards on all sides. An ideal choice for siting a treehouse.

Nesta Brohier comes of an old Dutch burgher family. A hundred years ago her grandfather purchased the New Oriental Hotel in Galle, an old Portuguese fort and harbour on the south-western tip of the island then called Ceylon, now Sri Lanka. Now in her eighties, Nesta is as vigorous as ever, constantly at work in the lovely tropical garden she has created behind the rambling hotel, which was once a barracks for Portuguese officers. It was as she was pruning back a purple bougainvillea and picking some anthurium blooms for the hotel that she recalled the treehouse she and her late husband built on their tea estate at Hewagama during the war years.

The best tea in Sri Lanka comes from the hill country around Nuwara Eliya, where, at altitudes of 5,000–6,000 feet, the steeply sloping hillsides, often shrouded in cool mist, create ideal conditions. When Nesta and her husband moved to Hewagama, to a bungalow fronted by a sweeping lawn, with a superb view across to Adams Peak, there in the centre of the lawn was a magnificent rain tree. Nesta took one look at it and knew instantly what had to be done.

'It was more a platform than a house – although there was a canopy overhead in case of an unexpected downpour. The platform was quite large. It could hold easily a dozen people. We fixed rungs onto the trunk of the rain tree, which fortunately sloped inwards. We climbed up as you might climb up the side of a ship. There were tables and chairs . . . we often had three tables for "bridge". Down below there was a large bed of anthurium, very convenient for tossing empty drink bottles overboard.' She smiled, 'And, my dear, we did drink a lot in those days, I suppose. We often carried a wind-up gramophone onto the lawn and danced up the tree. There was a dumb-waiter worked on a pulley for hauling up the drinks to the thirsty guests!'

The great days of the treehouse were during the latter years of the war, when Mountbatten made his HQ at Peradeniya. 'All those pretty Wrens and young naval officers coming up here on leave and wanting to enjoy themselves, and how they did, my dear,' she winked, 'up in the foliage of that rain tree.'

Nesta was justly proud of the garden she planted at Hewagama. There were lots of animals too, to keep her busy: muscovy ducks and fallow deer. 'My dear, we had bullock races and elephant races! The treehouse was the grandstand, everyone up there cheering the elephants on and placing bets. And race they did – steered by their yelling mahouts, although the result could be unpredictable, especially if one of them spotted a tasty palm leaf and veered off course.'

Another Brohier pet of that era was a giant python that lived in 'biblical' splendour up the rain tree, attached by a long chain. It was thick as a palm tree and almost as long. 'Quite harmless really, but sometimes guests were a bit dismayed by its sudden appearance coiling around the branches below as they scampered aloft.'

Apart from the grandstand view of elephant-racing, the treehouse also offered a marvellous outlook towards the spectacular Adams Peak, soaring 9,000 feet into the sky. Adams Peak is a strange, rocky pinnacle and on its summit is a giant footprint, reputedly that of Adam or Buddha – depending on one's religious preference.

The traditional way to climb Adams Peak is to leave the village of Dalhouse at 2 a.m. and climb up the thousands of steps cut into the rock, so as to reach the summit at dawn, when the rising sun casts a mysterious, perfectly triangular shadow of the peak against the opposite sky. At that moment Buddhist priests chant prayers, and temple musicians play their flutes and beat drums.

Nesta's treehouse was an ideal rendezvous for excursions to climb Adams Peak and a good excuse for a party. She also recalls with especial sympathy a treehouse party for the officers of the aircraft carrier *Courageous* before it set out on its last, ill-fated voyage when it was torpedoed and sunk with all hands.

After Independence, the tea estates were nationalized and Nesta and her husband returned to manage the New Oriental Hotel in Galle. Sadly the treehouse at Hewagama no longer exists. The rain tree grew too vast, and its great roots threatened the foundations of the bungalow. So down it went, and the treehouse with it.

But where one goes, another takes it place. A Cambridge undergraduate studying primatology recently returned from a wildlife sanctuary at Parambitulam, near Tunnakadan in the Kerala province of South India. Here the guest house, complete with bedrooms, bathrooms and verandah, has been built among the branches of a giant rain tree – presumably an ideal location for studying the habits of monkeys at home among the treetops.

A rather delightful footnote to this section happily came my way just as the manuscript was going to press. It comes from Sarah Holloway who works for the Leonard Cheshire Foundations and tours the Third World on its behalf. Writing from India, she says, 'I have found and been in a real treehouse. It is built between two Banyan trees on the golf course in Dehra Dun, Uttar Pradesh, Pradesh in North India. The downstairs is a small bar – complete with pre-war telephone. I'm not quite sure where the phone goes to or why! The upstairs is a little house and you go up steps around the trunk of the tree to get into it and it is really built around the branches! As it is a military golf course, strictly no admittance to the public, but I was able to see it c/o the Major General (Rtd.) Hakshi, who runs the Raphael Centre and took me to golf.'

A golf clubhouse up a banyan tree – what next?!

The Great Tree Arbour

In the Royal Botanical Gardens at Peradeniya in Sri Lanka is a *Ficus Benjamensis* planted in 1917 when my grandfather H. F. MacMillan was curator. The tree has spread out its limbs to create a massive bower some sixty yards in diameter and about fifteen to twenty feet high. Around the edges, the limbs are propped up to permit easy entry. Mr Sumithraarachchi, the present curator, estimates the area of this 'Umbrella Bower' to be about 1,800 square yards, and there must be room for a couple of thousand people to sit inside it — scope for the largest tree party ever. My grandfather's tree has become a favourite picnic spot — I counted over fifty families there.

This is not the end of the story, for Mr Sumithraarachchi says that in the Botanical Gardens at Calcutta a similar tree, a *Ficus Bengalensis* (related to our fig tree) has spread to create an arbour of over four acres. Originally one tree, the down-hanging roots have established themselves to create more trunks to support this massive dome of vegetation. The curator told me that this is probably the biggest tree in area and certainly the biggest bower anywhere in the world.

On a somewhat smaller scale, in the botanical gardens at Hahgalla, 6,000 feet up in the mountains of Sri Lanka, a small grove of *Cupressus Macrocarpa* has been trained to create a small tree arbour some ten feet across.

The Highest Treehouse in the World

Pemberton lies in the south-west corner of Western Australia. Surrounded by eucalyptus forest as far as the eye can see, it is a one-street logging town comprising two petrol stations, a general store and a sawmill.

Fires are a hazard in any forest but, because of the inflammable nature of gum trees, the karri forests around Pemberton are among the most vulnerable in the world. Apart from that, some of the tallest trees in the whole of Australia grow there, and one of these, a giant karri 300 years old and 60 metres tall, carries at its very tip a fire lookout cabin. Named 'the Gloucester tree' on account of a visit the late Duke of Gloucester paid it in 1947, the fire lookout tree is nowadays open to the public — or at any rate to those members of the public brave or reckless enough to climb the 200 vertical feet, rung by rung up the trunk, with not even a handrail to cling to and only the branches below to hide some of the drop.

The highest treehouse in the world. Two hundred feet high and still growing. It was named the Gloucester Tree after a Royal visit to Pemberton, Western Australia, in 1947

The cabin itself is a two-storey affair built around the trunk of the tree. It consists of a circular platform with a wooden plank floor and a steel cage around the edge. A trapdoor gives access to the upper floor, the lookout, with its compass and aids to pinpointing fires. When asked to describe the view, Helen Applegarth, a sculptress from Canterbury who had just climbed up with her boyfriend, was a bit bemused. She gazed over the sea of forest spreading to the horizon. 'Trees' she said gamely. 'Oh, and birds. Have you seen the kookaburras? They're a bit like big tatty kingfishers. And they've got this mocking cry.'

The mocking cry accompanies you as you make the descent down 252 rungs to *terra firma* far below. After the swaying tree cabin 200 feet up in the treetops, stepping onto solid ground is a bit like stepping off a ship: it takes a moment or two getting used to. An Australian commented sagely, 'Mate, in case you get really terrified during the descent, remember there's a loo at the bottom.' Helen proudly brandished the certificate she got from the petrol station in Pemberton, which stated clearly that she had climbed to the highest treehouse in the world!

John Morland's treehouse tree. A treehouse nightmare or the shape of things to come?

Fantasy Treehouses

Rock-a-bye-baby on the tree top,
When the wind blows, the cradle will rock,
When the bough bends, the cradle will fall,
Down comes the baby, cradle and all.

attributed to Charles Dupee Blake, 1846–1903

The fantasy possibilities of hollow trees have always caught man's imagination. In our fairy tales, hollow trees, toadstools and underground burrows become peopled with twinkly-eyed dwarfs, friendly bears and a whole anthropomorphic world.

Readers of Beatrix Potter may remember the plight of poor little Timothy Tiptoes who was squeezed and shoved into a little opening in a hollow tree by the squirrels, and left. There he finds himself in a home of Chipmunk, who kindly puts Timmy to bed and proceeds to feed him with the nuts that his wife, Goody Tiptoes, had poured down the woodpecker's hole. Unfortunately Timmy gets so fat that he is unable to get out again. He's not sure if he wants to: even in an imaginery sense, hollow trees offer all of us a sense of security from the blasts of reality.

The mythical treehouse world is a theme that has preoccupied the Glastonbury artist John Morland. Glastonbury itself may be partly responsible. The famous Tor capped by a solitary tower, visible for miles, is, according to the town sign, 'the Ancient Isle of Avalon'. It is as if you are crossing the frontier into a land of legend – the realm of King Arthur, where Excalibur lies gleaming under the murky waters of the long-lost lake, waiting to be retrieved, and magician Merlin still holds mysterious sway.

There is no doubt that the town, with an eye to its tourist potential, pushes this image for all it is worth – which is quite a lot. A local newspaper, *Glastonbury Commentator*, 'the Alternative Life Style Newspaper', is crammed with snippets of otherworldly information provided by 'The Goddess Column', 'The Woodcraft Folk' and 'The Green Compost Group'. There are possibly more self-employed witches, palm-readers, pagan priestesses and spiritualists in Glastonbury than anywhere else in the kingdom, but there is certainly nothing whatsoever freaky about John Morland who, together with his wife Jan, runs the Morland Galleries, an elegant emporium of Portmeirion china, framed watercolours, herbs, souvenirs and suchlike.

John Morland, tall and rather reserved, has been painting and engraving for years. His treehouse fantasies date from his experiences at the hands of the National Health Service. His poster 'The Hospital Tree' was his own therapeutic way of giving vent to all his exasperation. The detail is brilliant and not without humour: myriads of robot figures, cooks, surgeons, nurses, porters, all identical in appearance and all busily 'beavering' away expressionlessly at their appointed tasks and getting in one another's way. The different levels of the tree are occupied by waiting-rooms, laundries, bathrooms, wards and operating theatres, with little figures spiralling up from one to the next until finally the patients emerge into the sunshine and the balconies among the branches at the top.

The sequel to the Hospital Tree poster was John Morland's 'Treehouses' where everything from a parish church to a Chinese pagoda gets hoisted aloft into the boughs.

The essential difference between this mythical treehouse world and any other is that John Morland has turned the idea on its head and politicized treehouses from being bastions of freedom and eccentricity into communes inhabited by automata with no obvious independent will of their own. There is a Hieronymous Bosch quality to his drawing, bizarre, fascinating and frightening at the same time. Not that the drawings lack humanity, but like the London underground at rush hour they are crowded and somewhat bewildering.

Jan Morland likens Glastonbury to a world of 'upward moving spiralists'. Was that what her husband's treehouse world is all about too? The only problem is what to do once one has reached the top. Jump? Later, as I climbed the steep Tor, joining and passing scattered bands of tourists spiralling their way haphazardly upwards, I felt almost happy to be human.

John Morland's hospital tree

J. R. R. Tolkien, Professor of English at Oxford was another man who lived largely in a fantasy world of his own creation. Writing in the rather bleak brick surrounds of his Oxford garage he invented all manner of unusual dwellings and dining places for his varied and versatile characters. His heroes were Hobbits or Halflings, little short, stout, furry humanoids who — like the celebrated Badger in *The Wind in the Willows* — preferred living in underground burrows. During their prodigous exploits in *The Lord of the Rings* trilogy, the Hobbits are forced to seek the help and alliance of Elves who live in virtual cities high up in the trees. Tolkien describes how the Hobbits approach the Elven city of the Galadhrim — a green hill thronged with Mallorn trees of great height standing up against the twilight like towers, with countless lamps gleaming in the many-tiered branches. As the Hobbits enter the wood they hear voices drifting down through the canopy of leaves. On being summoned to do so, they enter the city by climbing up long ladders which have been let down, and they discover platforms or 'flets' arranged on each side of the boles of the trees. Some are even built right around the trunk with the ladder passing through them. Tolkien leaves us to imagine the detailed construction for ourselves — but the inference is that walls and roofs are made by interlacing branches. Finally the weary Hobbits — who are happier with their feet firmly on the ground — reach a wide platform — a *talan*, as big as the deck of a great ship. On the middle of this is a house large enough even for men to live in. A reminder that Hobbits were shorter than pigmies! In this house perched on the top of the tallest Mallorn tree the Hobbits are entertained by the hospitable elves, and although they initially regard the food and drink offered with some suspicion, they quickly come to appreciate its sustaining and nourishing qualities. The elves' *lembas* or waybread, which they take with them on their departure, serves them in much the same way as the concentrated foodstuffs used by modern astronauts.

On the other side of the world another teacher, James Baxter, was also intrigued by treehouses. James K. Baxter, was a teacher at a primary school in the Hutt Valley, New Zealand, and he wrote poems for his classes to use. He wrote them for 'the in-betweeners, the ones who are neither infants nor fully literate'. The themes sprang up in part from the children's conversations — about animals, boats, railway trains, houses on fire, conditions of weather — and in part from his own memories of childhood. When he stopped being a teacher, he set the poems aside, partly because, as he admitted, he had no more need for them, and partly because they were not 'literary works'. One can imagine how his pupils enjoyed the following poem which he wrote during the 1960s:

> John and Judith
> And Billy and me,
> We have our own house
> In a willow tree.
>
> It's built of boards
> And battens and tin
> From the packing case
> That the tractor came in.
>
> Up the slippery trunk
> Of the tree we climb
> With a rope to help us,
> One at a time;
>
> But once we're up
> And safe inside
> Only the wind knows
> Where we hide.
>
> Down in the paddock
> The brown horse neighs
> And in stormy weather
> The whole house sways
>
> Like a ship at sea
> While the branches roar
> And birds fly past
> At the open door.

In 1974, Joanna Stubbs wrote and illustrated a delightful book for children called *The Tree House*. In this tree Emily, Matthew and Timothy played at pirates, kings and queens and shops all summer. However, before they could move in, they had to do a lot of work.

In the tree there was a house ... with a window, a door and a ladder made of rope to climb up and look inside.

They called it 'The Chestnuts'. It needed quite a lot doing to it. They mended the holes with wood and a hammer and nails. They swept out the old brown leaves and feathers and dust. They found a piece of corrugated plastic to put on the roof. They even painted the walls inside. And when all that was done they brought the furniture; an orange box, a lamp their mother had thrown away and, best of all, an armchair, very old but comfortable, which they found discarded in a shed. Tim wheeled it up the hill in a wheelbarrow. That was hard work, but not as hard as climbing up the rope ladder with it.

And then they moved in. They slept at home each night. But nearly every day they brought sandwiches to the house and played in the tree. No one else knew the secret. Except for the birds and animals, who soon got used to the children.

Other children's books of earlier years involving treehouses include several stories by Enid Blyton, *Hollow Tree House* and *The Magic Faraway Tree*. 'Its name is the Enchanted Wood,' said Jo [in Enid Blyton's *The Magic Faraway Tree*],

Up in the Milly-Molly-Mandy nest. Lots of children's stories of the twenties included treehouse romps

'and in the middle is the most wonderful tree in the world. It goes right up to the clouds — and at the top it is always some strange land. You can go there by climbing up to the top branch of the Faraway Tree, going up a little ladder through a hole in the big cloud that always lies on the top of the tree — and there you are in some peculiar land.'

A number of children's books were published during the 1920s involving treehouse adventures, including *More of Milly-Molly-Mandy* by Joyce Lankester Brisley — a mildly unnerving title for today's adult reader. Milly-Molly-Mandy is quite an organizer. The entire family gets roped in to assist with the furnishing of her snug tree nest:

> Then Grandma came across the meadow bringing some old cushions, and she tied them to the end of the rope, and little-friend-Susan pulled them up and arranged them on the carpet.
>
> Then Aunty came along, and she tied a little flower vase on the end of a rope, and Milly-Molly-Mandy pulled it up and set it in the middle of the table. And now the Milly-Molly-Mandy nest was properly furnished, and Milly-Molly-Mandy was in such a hurry to get Billy Blunt to come and see it that she could hardly get down from it quickly enough.

The book is very prettily illustrated by the author, but full-blooded men are advised to grit their teeth and watch their blood pressure before tackling some parts of this childhood classic.

An enchanted wood that few of us ever tire of is that inhabited by Pooh Bear and his friends. In this world of Pooh Corner just about everyone seems to live in or up trees. Owl has a splendid treetop residence. Christopher Robin lived in a hollow tree at the very top of the Forest. He, Piglet and Pooh are always in and out of each other's arboreal abodes: Pooh frequently getting stuck as a result of stealing too much honey!

A favourite cartoon character — Asterix, similarly favours living a safe distance above ground level. In *Asterix and the Normans* his main dwelling is a spacious timbered hall set on top of a decapitated oak tree.

Edward Lear's limericks included anything that rhymed and tree was a natural choice. Thus we get the tale of the Old Man in a Tree.

Christopher Robin's treehouse. Note the spiral staircase and the little window

> There was an Old Man in a Tree,
> Whose Whiskers were lovely to see;
> But the Birds of the Air
> Pluck'd them perfectly bare,
> To make themselves Nests in that Tree.
>
> Edward Lear

Fantasy Treehouses

Perhaps this was the inspiration for his later treetop epic – *The Quangle Wangle's Hat* where just about every character he ever invented gathers on the top of the Crumpetty Tree where the Quangle Wangle sat complaining, 'very few people come this way'.

> But there came to the Crumpetty Tree,
>   Mr. and Mrs. Canary;
> And they said, – 'Did ever you see
>   'Any spot so charmingly airy?
> 'May we build a nest on your lovely Hat?
> 'Mr. Quangle Wangle, grant us that!
> 'O please let us come and build a nest
> 'Of whatever material suits you best,
>   'Mr. Quangle Wangle Quee!'
>
> And the Golden Grouse came there,
>   And the Pobble who has no toes, –
> And the small Olympian bear, –
>   And the Dong with a luminous nose.
> And the Blue Baboon, who played the flute, –
> And the Orient Calf from the Land of Tute, –
> And the Attery Squash, and the Bisky Bat, –
> All came and built on the lovely Hat
>   Of the Quangle Wangle Quee.

On the top of the Crumpetty Tree. Lear deposited his entire cast of poetic characters in it

In classical literature, one can scour the pages of Chaucer, Dante, Milton for references to treehouses without success. The Bible hasn't a word to say for them, and Shakespeare only a passing reference in *Twelfth Night* when Viola exclaims, 'Make me a willow cabin at your gate . . .'

Even Daniel Defoe ignores the potential of a treehouse in *Robinson Crusoe*, and it wasn't until J. R. Wyss wrote the hugely popular *Swiss Family Robinson* in 1813 that treehouses became immortalized in literature.

The Swiss Family Robinson concerns the amazing adventures of a minister, his wife and four sons, Fritz, Ernest, Francis and Jack, after they are shipwrecked and cast up on a desert island. They are able to rescue some indispensables from the ship, but they survive largely on their own ingenuity in making use of everything they find on the island. They construct a wonderful house in a large tree where they are safe from wild animals, and are so content with their island life that they refuse to leave when a ship finally comes to their rescue.

More of this book later when we come to the chapter on building your own treehouse!

In 1917, the American writer Edgar Rice Burroughs published the first book in that immensely popular saga 'Tarzan'. Since then the story has been the basis for countless Hollywood movies. A recurrent theme in all of them is to see Tarzan – the white man who has been brought up by apes – swinging through the trees on long creepers, uttering his frightening call as he comes to the rescue. He is also depicted as living in a spacious treehouse. With cinematographic licence, Hollywood can do anything. The actual story is slightly different. Tarzan is the son of Lord and Lady Greystoke who are set down on a remote West African beach when the crew of the *Fuwalda*, the barquentine they are sailing on, mutinies. Lord Greystoke does build a temporary treehouse – as is described later in the 'Build your own Treehouse' chapter, but this is principally to provide a refuge from the wild beasts of the forest while he completes a more substantial cabin. It is in this cabin that Tarzan is born, rescued by the apes when his parents die, and to which he constantly returns as he seeks to establish his own identity.

Major Charles Gibson may have taken a tip or two from Edgar Rice Burroughs when he wrote 'The Wizard King',

Fantasy Treehouses

'Pon my soul, I never thought I would live to make the acquaintance of a man who lived in a tree,' said Wynne.
A sketch from The Wizard King

serialized in *The Boys' Own Paper* 1920 (Volume XL, part III). In this story a band of explorers are seeking clues to the disappearance of an earlier expedition in hostile jungle territory.

> ... a moment after they were devouring plantains [bananas] with the voracity of hungry wolves. In the midst of this feast they were startled by a loud voice, and looking up they beheld a man with a long white beard who addressed them in perfect English.
>
> 'You trespass on my preserves,' said he ... He led the way for some distance along the bank of the river until at last they came to a place where a limb of forest jutted forth to the margin of the water. Here was a clump of the most gigantic trees and Mellors and his companions were astonished when they beheld, hanging down the trunk of one of these trees a kind of rope ladder which had been very cleverly constructed out of the pliable, ropelike stems of a species of creeping plant that was plentiful in the forest.
>
> About forty feet from the ground the great branches of the tree were forked in the shape of a cup, and in the angle thus formed, occupying an area of about six square yards, a rude hut had been constructed, built of wood and thatched with the dried leaves of palm trees, placed one on top of the other, very close together in much the same manner as a roof is slated or tiled.
>
> Climbing up the rope ladder they found themselves in a chamber which was as ingenious as its site was original.
>
> Though within there was plenty of room for the four of them, it was apparent at a glance that every effort had been made to economise space; there was a rifle rack and a folding table attached by hinges to the walls. These hinges were of untanned leather – obviously the skin of some wild animal, a rhinoceros or an elephant. The bed consisted of four rough pieces of wood, forming a rectangle across which strips of the same kind of leather had been attached, thus forming a mattress similar to that used by the South African Boers. This bed could be hoisted to the ceiling and lowered at will. Upon the shelves were packages of rifle ammunition and a box of shot-gun cartridges. There were many other things such as one would little expect to find in the midst of the wilderness – a clinometer, a prismatic compass, a few books on tropical botany and several carpenter's tools, everything in fact which Costello had been able to save from the illfated Davis Expedition.
>
> 'This,' said Wynne, 'is unique. 'Pon my soul, I never thought I would live to make the acquaintance of a man who lived in a tree!'

Build Your Own Treehouse

Treehouses are not like other buildings. There is no fixed plan to follow when constructing them. They are something you tend to make up as you go along. In fact, this flexibility of approach is very important. Treehouses are adapted according to the site, the tree available, the materials you have to build with, and what the individual builder has in mind.

Most of us conceive an idea for a treehouse from seeing a film featuring one, or reading a description in a book. It is something that appeals to the escapist in us. But, as we have already seen, tree platforms and treehouses are put to a variety of uses. They may also, for instance, be regarded as extensions of garden landscaping, in much the same way as pergolas, bowers and summerhouses. In countries where hunting is popular, treehouses are very likely to be built with the idea of a 'hide' in mind. In this case the aim will be to make them as inconspicuous as possible. In other cases they are intended to be clearly visible, as was Pitchford's *'trompe l'œil'* treehouse.

Considering the present popularity of barbecues, it is surprising that treehouses for this sort of entertainment have not caught on. Patio barbecues are dependent on the weather, but move the venue a few feet out into the garden, and a few feet up into the trees, and a whole new fresh and more appealing ambience is created. A large, sturdy platform with a simple tent roof will suffice. Even if it does drizzle everyone stays dry and can continue to enjoy the *al fresco* evening. And the treeplatform does not have to be very high up. It is amazing what a difference simply a few feet above ground make,

Pooh Bear visiting Owl's old world residence of great if misspelt charm

combined with the effect of some trailing branches and rambling creepers.

Advice: Strong handrails and handy bucket of sand or a fire-extinguisher.

The following ground rules come from a Forestry Commission spokesman. However, like all instructions, some are easier said than done. (See item 5.)

Building tips
1. Choose a tree that is mature and well-leafed. Avoid beech and elm; English oak and fruit trees are best.
2. Check for disease, rot or pockets of water – they are signs of decay.
3. Build platforms on forks close to the trunk, not out on long branches.
4. Try not to use nails; they cause wounds and invite disease.
5. Lash platforms into place with nylon rope. It can be eased periodically to allow for tree growth.
6. Soft wood is best for the platform. Industrial pallets are cheap and ready-made. Shape or pad the edges to avoid scarring the tree.
7. Keep the structure lightweight. Use exterior-grade or marine plywood for the walls, treated hardboard for the roof, and polythene or perspex for the windows. Weatherproof with wood preservative or glass paint.
8. For maximum safety build the house about six feet from the ground and make safety rails for young children.
9. Use a ladder for access. Never nail rungs to a tree; remember, you'll want to enjoy the tree long after the treehouse has gone.
10. Check both the tree and its house frequently.

Planning permission
A treehouse that recently fell foul of the local planning authority was one built by Matthew and Tom Clayton of Fleets Road, Sturton-by-Stow in Lincolnshire. By the time they had completed the treehouse thirteen feet up among the boughs of an old apple tree at the bottom of their garden, they were justly proud of it. It had glazed windows, wall-to-wall carpeting and plenty of wall shelves. It also overlooked the neighbour's garden who complained to the West Lindsey

Ralph Curry's residence among the treetops near Canterbury is largely supported on telegraph poles, which also make up many of the construction units. Ralph is unashamedly a 'wood butcher'. Eight-inch screws hammered home is his answer to joints

District Council that the treehouse gave the boys a clear view into her kitchen! The local officials arrived, got out their tape measures, and declared that the treehouse was 4.4 metres above ground level – 0.4 metres over the limit a garden building can be erected without planning approval! It must either be pulled down or architectural plans submitted for Planning Committee consent.

Fortunately for the boys, their father, Ivan Clayton was on their side. Even more fortunate was the fact that he was a lecturer in art and design. Mr Clayton set about producing the necessary plans and specifications, drawings of different elevations and all the other relevant and irrelevant details so beloved by officialdom. He submitted the drawings and the application together with a £45 fee to the Planning Department.

It was like that old BBC radio series, *Toytown*, all over again. The Planning Officer scrutinized the plans, the Planning Subcommittee inspected the site and deliberated, the local press got hold of the story and came to take photographs, the local constabulary deliberated, the Town Council deliberated, the Mayor (in this case Chairman) deliberated until finally a decision worthy of the Wisdom of Solomon was reached. The treehouse could stay if the boys agreed to black out the windows with the view into the neighbour's kitchen. Nobody mentioned that by just climbing the tree they could have the same view if they wanted. There was no law to stop them doing that! Otherwise the Town Council might have decided they had to climb the tree blindfold!

The windows have now been painted over and one hopes neighbourly relations have been restored. Meanwhile the West Lindsey District Council are probably relieved to have less weighty matters to consider: education, rates, etc., etc.

So be warned – don't build your treehouse higher than four metres. But what if you build it at this height and then the tree goes on growing? What has the law to say about that?

Choice of tree
Nothing beats a good solid spreading oak. The following is an extract from a treehouse story in the *Ecology Magazine* sent to me by its editor:

> One day, as we breasted the steep hill that took us plunging down into the valley, there at the bottom amongst the spreading limbs

The Downings' moated treehouse under construction at their farm near Chediston, Suffolk. The treehouse began as a centre prop for the twin suspension bridges linking the island and then it grew. Partly supported on piles and partly by tree, John Downing used only good cured hardwood timber. He intends bridges and treehouse to last. Joints, joists, etc., were all built to the highest specification

of a giant oak we saw a weird contraption covered in a skin of brightly coloured sail cloth. Curious we crossed the field which took us down to the river and peered upwards to a precarious-looking structure which creaked and groaned as the tree swayed in the wind. To get to his home the fellow had rigged up a simple ladder with slates nailed across a single pole. This fishbone-like structure was suspended from a sturdy branch, and having scaled it, he next had to haul himself up onto the branch and then a few steps more up the trunk. His home really was for the birds. He had banged some 4 × 2s across the space where the branches spread and had laid a few planks across. The canvas was stretched all round but it flapped in the wind like a loose sail. For his bed he had hauled up some soap boxes on which he had laid a mattress; beyond that there was just enough room to stand. What staggered us was his dexterity in getting up and down, which he could do in pitch black with a Cornish gale swirling through the branches. Only once, after a particularly fiendish night, did he admit to some anxiety, 'Oak trees don't blow over, do they?' he asked.

Horse-chestnuts are often avoided as they have a tendency to shed limbs. If you are in the fortunate position of having a variety of trees to choose from to build a treehouse in, obviously one with low, spreading boughs is the easiest. An invariable problem is that a tree that is pretty to look at is usually difficult to build in – branches get in the way of walls and roof beams. You are then faced with the choice of chopping off the intruding boughs or adapting the construction. Usually a compromise is reached: a branch is lopped away here, and the design is adapted there.

An advantage of building a treehouse among the trees but not entirely supported by them is that your construction can be independent of them. In this case telegraph poles or strong chestnut beams are ideal supports. Chestnut is one of the most rot-resistant woods. In Italy, chestnut poles are used to support electricity cables in rural areas. Chestnut beams, even without any preservative, can last for a long time. The usual method of preservation is to paint creosote on the part of the poles to be buried. Another way to protect them is by charring the surface in a fire. This also keeps mould at bay.

Obviously the farther above ground-level this kind of structure is, the more it is prone to sway. Hence the advantage of mooring it to at least one sturdy tree. Also, angled supports sledgehammered into the ground will reduce movement.

Ralph Curry (p. 81) has a friend in Wales who simply hoisted a hut up a tree on ropes and pulleys, attaching other guy ropes to the four corners to stop it swaying about too much!

Bearing in mind the people who build tree platforms among the palms of the Orinoco delta, if you are fortunate enough to own a copse of conifers, pines, larches, spruce – anything will do – judicious thinning will leave good upright poles six feet apart, an ideal space to erect a platform.

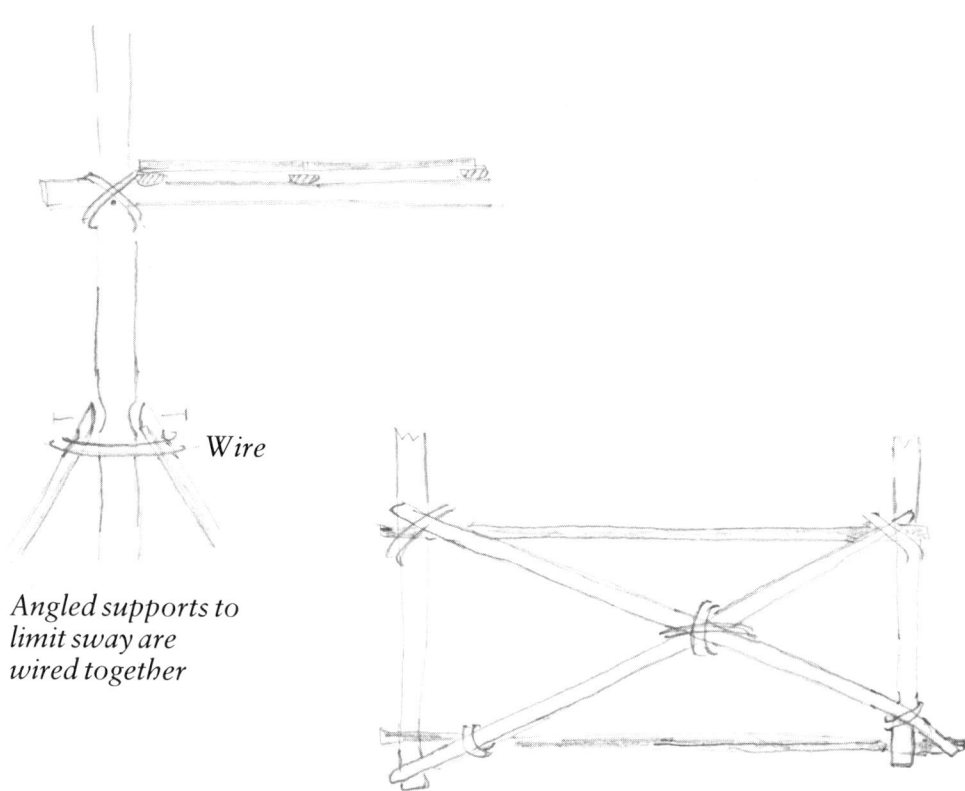

Angled supports to limit sway are wired together

Frame held together by crossmembers and wired

Angled supports and frame

The platform
The frame of the platform should be built of sturdy, seasoned, unpliable wood. Poles left out a single season will lose their springyness and become more suitable.

There are various ways to attach the outer frame of the platform to the tree, or the pole supports.

1. The platform may rest like a raft on the spreading branches. In this case a whole cat's-cradle of beams may be required to provide a suitable level frame on which to nail the flooring planks.

2. The platform may have to be fixed to upright supports — trees or poles. In this case, cut a deep notch in the upright and fit the cross member into the notch with six inch nails or better

still a long bolt. (Wood-boring augurs can be obtained up to three feet long.) If you are using only nails, it is advisable to support the crossmember with an extra block nailed into the upright just below it.

The main objection to binding living boughs with ropes or wire etc is that these cut into the tree. They are also very difficult to loosen later, especially considering the weight of the treehouse. In time they will appear to be buried in the bark,

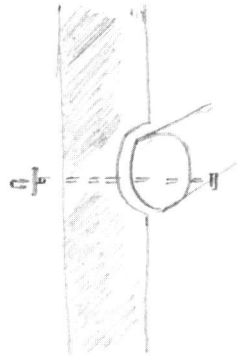
Slots and bolts are best

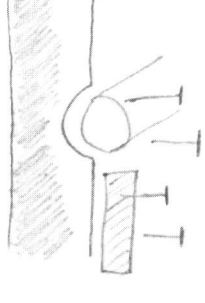
Nailed crossmembers can be supported

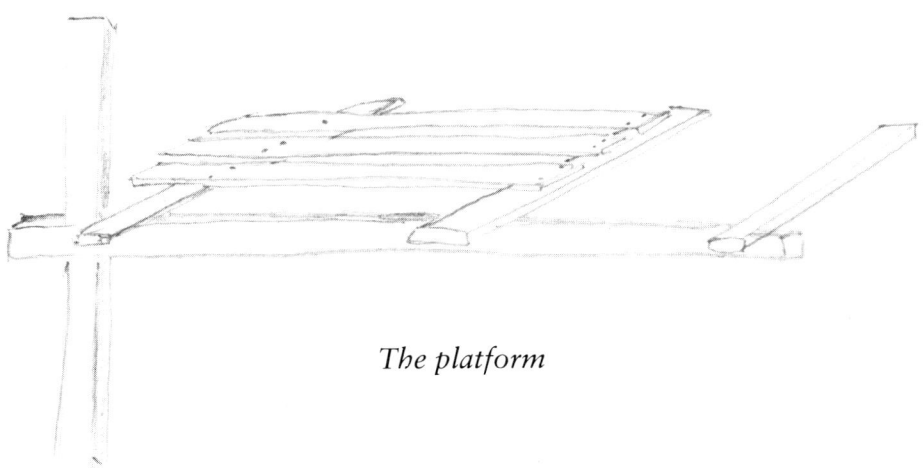
The platform

but in fact they may strangle the sap flow and gradually cause die-back and the eventual death of the tree.

The platform frame will consist of a square of sturdy poles across which lighter beams are fixed at yard intervals. The flooring planks can be nailed over this.

The bigger the platform, the more space there will be on which to manœuvre when building the hut. Also the extra space will make an excellent verandah.

The hut's frame

The frame of the hut may be there already if the platform was erected between existing straight trees or upright poles. In this case it will be much easier adding the walls and the roof.

If the platform rests on spreading boughs, a completely separate hut frame is required. This should consist of squared lengths of timber. Softwood is easier to work and cheaper. For the main struts three inches by three is the minimum. It is important to remember that not only will the frame have to carry the walls and the roof, but you may also wish it to support an 'attic' platform for storage or sleeping.

The roof

Having established four cornerposts, the next thing to build is the roof. To construct a sloping roof there should be an upright post in the centre of two end walls supporting a ridge pole. The roof frame should extend beyond the hut walls to provide deep sheltering eaves. It is a good idea to continue the eaves right over the verandah.

The roof frame having been nailed in position, there are two main choices of waterproofing, corrugated iron, preferably sheets of galvanized tin or corrugated perspex, or a sheet of plywood or hardboard, covered with roofing felt (tar paper). This can be tacked down with broadheaded zinc tacks or, better still, thin wooden battens. To improve insulation a good idea is to thatch this with straw. Shred up a couple of straw bales and, having spread it over the roof, hold it in place with a nylon net of broad mesh, (the sort used to train sweet peas is ideal and virtually invisible). Every couple of seasons a new layer of straw may be added and another net. To prevent the straw rotting on the roofing felt, a layer of bamboo poles can be first placed in position. South Sea island huts are built

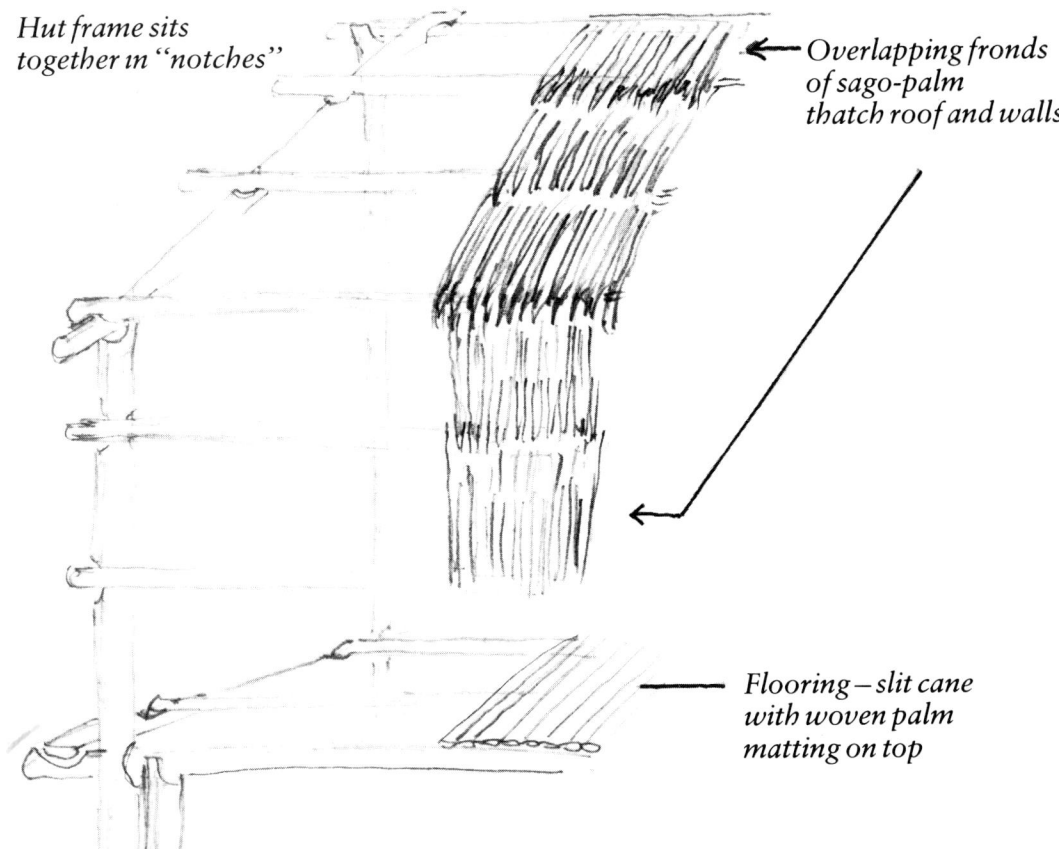

Hut frame and thatching

without a single nail. Beams and struts fit into cut-out notches. Overlapping palm fronds last up to five years before replacement. Where coconut fronds are used, for example in Sri Lanka, they must be replaced every year. Coconut fronds have to be soaked for two days and are then woven together. It is a good idea to insulate the corrugated roof from the inside with a layer of felt.

The space created above head height by the sloping roof can be utilized into a half attic, with a removable ladder, ideal for storing folding chairs etc or as a sleeping platform.

An appropriate quotation at this point is an extract from the beginning of Edgar Rice Burroughs' *Tarzan, Lord of the Apes*. John Clayton, Lord Greystoke, and his young bride,

Lady Alice (who will later become the parents of Tarzan), have just been set down on the savage coast by the mutinous crew of the *Fuwalda*:

> Clayton's first thought was to arrange a sleeping shelter for the night – something which might serve to protect them from the prowling beasts of prey.
>
> A hundred yards from the beach was a little level spot, fairly free of trees, and here they decided eventually to build a permanent house, but for the time being, they both thought it best to construct a little platform in the trees out of reach of the larger of the savage beasts in whose realm they were.
>
> Clayton selected four trees which formed a rectangle about eight feet square and cutting long branches from other trees he constructed a framework around them about ten feet from the ground, fastening the ends of the branches securely to the trees by means of rope . . .
>
> Across this framework Clayton placed other smaller branches quite close together. This platform he paved with the huge fronds of elephant's ear which grew in profusion about them, and over the fronds he laid a great sail folded into several thicknesses.
>
> Seven feet higher he constructed a similar though lighter platform to serve as roof, and from the sides of this he suspended the balance of his sailcloth for walls.
>
> When completed he had a rather snug little nest, to which he carried their blankets and some of their lighter luggage.

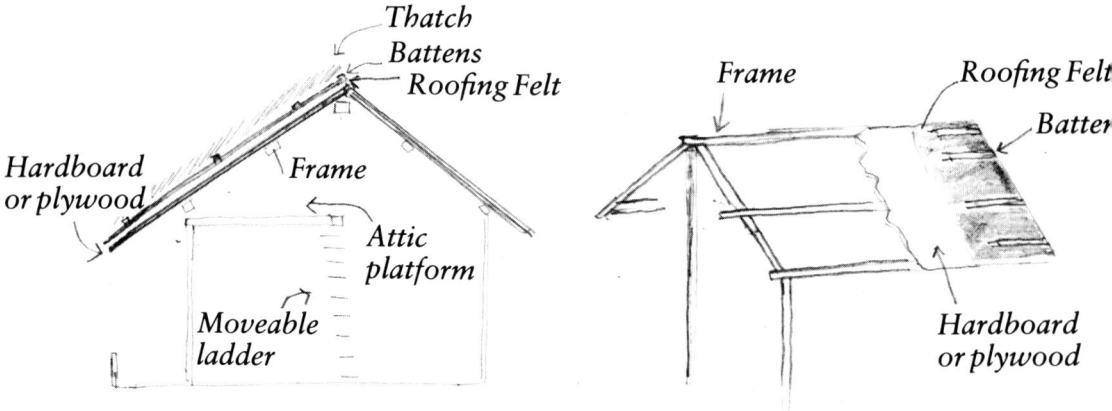

Roof construction

Access

One thing Edgar Rice Burroughs fails to mention is how to climb up. In Wyss's *Swiss Family Robinson*, the first thing the family did after being shipwrecked was to hoist a rope ladder into the trees and start hammering out a treehouse refuge.

> I then tied the end of my ball of thread to one of my arrows and sent it directly over one of the thickest of the lower branches of the tree . . .
>
> I hastened to complete my ladder, by two ropes of forty feet each. These I stretched on the ground at about one foot distance from the other. Fritz cut pieces of cane two feet long, which Ernest passed to me. I placed these in knots which I had made in the cords at about a foot distance from each other, and Jack fastened each end with a long nail to prevent it slipping. In a very short time our ladder was completed and tying it to the end of the cord which went over the branch we drew it up without difficulty.

Rope ladders also have the advantage of being able to be raised against savage beasts and unwelcome guests: 'I had detached the lower part from the roots where it was nailed, in order to be able to draw it up for the night. We were thus as safe in our castle as knights of old, when their drawbridge was raised.'

The Walkers devised a similar system for Treetops in Kenya after several guests had experienced close encounters of a not totally welcome kind with the animal visitors to the waterhole: 'Eventually the lower end of the 35ft ladder to our tree hotel was hinged like a kind of drawbridge. As soon as the party had climbed the ladder, the porters who had accompanied us turned a winch, raising the lower section by steel cable high into the branches. If, after the porters had gone, anyone wanted to go down to the ground again, we lowered him on the rope which passed over a pulley and was used for hoisting up water and baggage.'

There are various alternatives to rope ladders. The obvious one is a long builder's ladder, but if one of the rules of the treehouse designer is to pretend he or she is a castaway (even if the treehouse is in a suburban back garden), it is not very difficult to make a rustic ladder or stepway, from two parallel planks of wood, with small boards (one foot six inches) placed

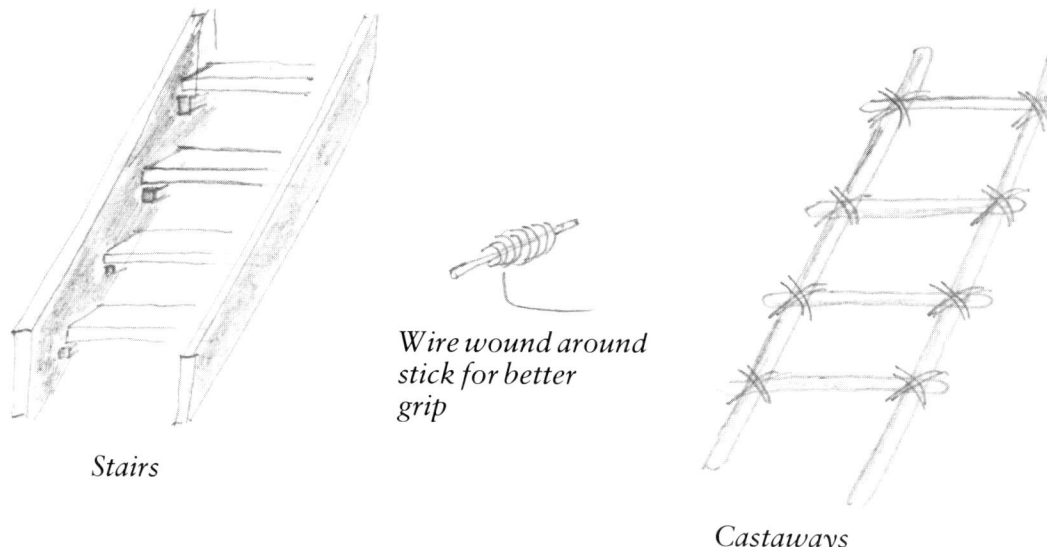

Stairs

Wire wound around stick for better grip

Castaways ladder

Ladders

like shelves on battens. (See sketch.) For a real ladder, fixing two long poles with the rungs not only nailed but also bound with wire is a good method. When binding with wire, remember to wear an old glove and to wind one yard lengths of wire onto a short length of stick: this will enable you to get a better grip and to pull the wire much tighter.

The hut walls
1. Strong frame.
2. Nail onto the outside overlapping fencing boards, and back this on the inside with hardboard or plywood. If you wish to use hardboard sheets on the outside, it is best to paint the shiny surface with 'tar varnish' (obtainable from ships' chandlers – cheap and practical.) An effective way to insulate the walls is to tack carpet underfelt over the inside, or old carpets turned around. The backing gives a tapestry finish to the walls and is good to pin decorations to.

Windows
Perspex sheets make good, strong, flexible windows and can be cut down to size with a hacksaw. They are especially good for large picture windows. Draughts can be eliminated around

the edges with felt and battens. For light, plus a double-glazing (insulation) effect, layers of stretched strong clear plastic sheeting can be thumbtacked (drawing-pinned) onto both sides of lengths of wooden trellis frames.

Doors
Old doors are not hard to find and can be sawn to size. Use good strong hinges and felt the frame edges to eliminate draughts.

Floors
Draughts and cold floors are two enemies of treehouse-dwellers. The best treatment is to line the floor with a large sheet of plastic and cover this with several layers of old carpets.

Heating
Gas stove – with large bottles of calor gas or butane gas. Treehouses tend to be small and snug, and warm up very quickly. A large gas bottle lasts for ages. For more durable heat plus a bit of character, nothing beats a wood stove or preferably a wood and coal stove. Ten kilo sacks of coal are easier to haul up and store than woodpiles.

There are plenty of old (or new) cast-iron stoves about these days. Even an old Rayburn cooker (make sure your floor is strong enough to support this monster!) is excellent for Sunday roasts, but you will need a pulley hoist to get it up into the treehouse. An old iron stove from British Rail guards' vans is fine if you can get hold of one. Remember that the more tin chimney piping is inside the hut, the better the heating, since the tin chimney pipe gets hot very quickly and acts as a radiator.

In some ways it is easier hauling up really heavy objects than lighter ones, because one is often tempted to try to lift things if it is at all possible, risking a strained back, slipping off the ladder or worse. If something is really heavy, you will have to tax your brain for an ingenious solution. Hence the virtue of a good pulley hoist from a nearby branch or attached to the treehouse frame itself.

The Swiss Family Robinson used a hoist to advantage: 'I carried with me a large pulley fixed to the end of a rope which I attached to a branch above us to enable us to raise the planks necessary to form the groundwork of our habitation. I smoothed the branches a little with my axe, sending the boys down to be out of the way . . .'

Wyss goes on to describe their progress:

> We set to work stoutly with axe and saw to rid ourselves of all useless branches. Some, about six feet above our foundations I left to suspend our hammocks from, and others, a little higher to support the roof which at present was to be merely sailcloth. My wife succeeded in collecting us some boards and planks (driftwood) which with her assistance and the aid of the pulley we hoisted up. We then arranged them on the level branches close to each other in such a manner as to form a smooth and solid floor. I made a sort of parapet around to prevent accidents. By degrees our dwelling began to assume a distinct form, the sailcloth was raised over the high branches forming a roof and being brought down on each side was nailed to the parapet. The immense trunk, protected the back of our apartment, and the front was open to admit the breeze from the sea. We hoisted our hammocks and blankets by the pulley and suspended them. And as our day was not yet exhausted we set about constructing a rude table and some benches which we placed between the roots of the tree, henceforward to be our dining-room.

Lighting

Italian children collect bottles of glow-worms in the summertime, and for a while these make a powerful lamp, but in our northern climate perhaps the two alternatives are either a direct cable from a house or a twelve-volt system based on twelve-volt re-chargeable batteries. Cheap old batteries are more trouble than they are worth, since you have to recharge them constantly. Get one that still holds its charge. A rule of thumb for durability is to add up the watts of your light bulbs and divide this into the ampere hours of your battery. Most batteries have roughly forty ampere hours. Caravan strip lights are good. They give off a lot of light and do not consume too much power.

Since batteries are heavy and awkward to carry, it may be a good idea to keep your battery in a large waterproofed box at the base of the tree and run wires up. If the lights dim suddenly and you can drive a car near to the tree, connect starter cables from car battery to treehouse battery, positive to positive etc.

To be fully independent it is possible to buy small wind-driven generators designed for yachts. Whenever the wind blows, these trickle-charge the battery. They are rather expensive. Perhaps a modern technique would be to erect a solar panel. However, a problem about treehouses is a lack of direct sunlight once the tree is in full summer leaf.

The modern treehouse-owner who wishes to floodlight his creation should not be faced with the problems that confronted the Walkers at Treetops in Kenya when they tried to supplement the moonlight with primitive attempts at floodlighting: 'We tried car spotlights and headlamps worked by a battery but they were too brilliant and except for the buffalo, most of the game ran away. Consequently we had to rely on natural light and visits to Treetops were restricted to a few days either side of the full moon.'

Water
A bilge pump from a boat shop can draw water up from ground-level. A plastic water-butt on the ground is easily refilled from a garden hose. Or alternatively – if the treehouse roof is of corrugated iron – rainwater could be collected via a gutter and run into the water butt. A bit of wire netting will stop most leaves being washed down, and a simple filter is not hard to make.

An excellent 'African village' filter was an oil drum with stones at the bottom, gravel above this, and a layer of sand on top. It was amazingly effective.

Communications
To be right up to date, fit an extension telephone, especially useful if the treehouse is being used as an office or a studio. If it's a den for the kids, a long piece of string with a bell on the end, or a tin with a stone rattling, does just as well. But if you are expecting important telephone calls and the house bell jangles, it may become perilous leaping down the ladder and racing across the slippery landscape.

An alternative is a CB radio, relatively inexpensive and very useful. If one channel is occupied, you can move over to another – except Channel 9, which is reserved for the Emergency Services. One can also listen in to all sorts of varied and unusual conversations from the locality and try to identify the voices – bear this in mind if you do intend to use

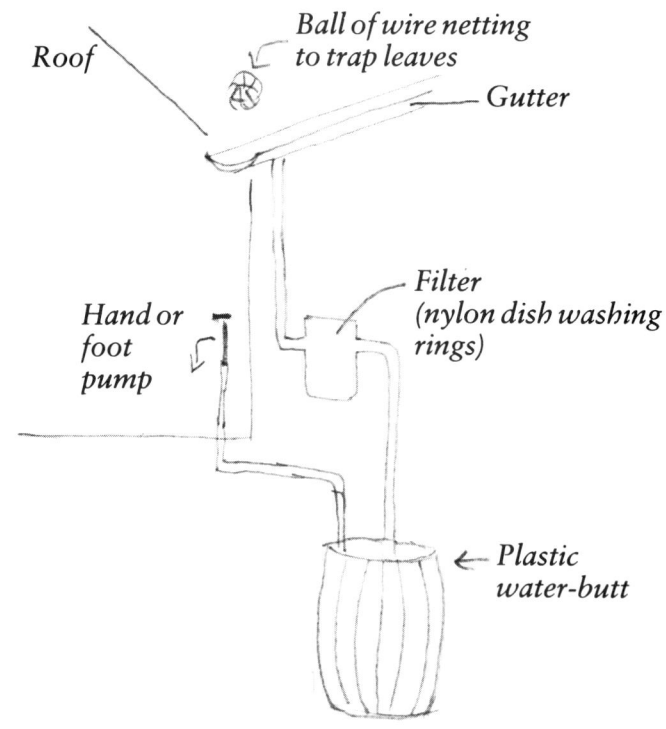

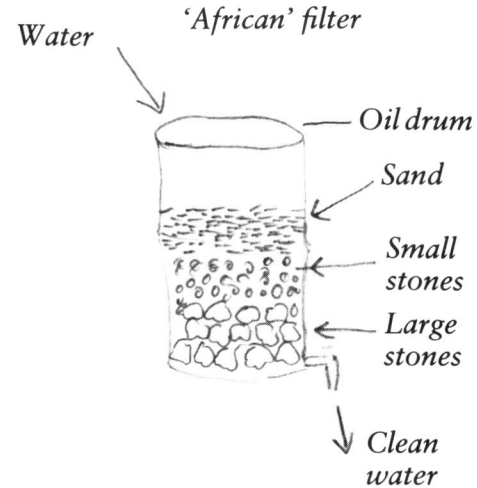

Water filter

CB as a private telephone, and avoid any obvious call signs or 'handles', otherwise the location of the treehouse may be inadvertently given away to unscrupulous listeners or potential thieves.

Other forms of communication include semaphore, morse, heliograph and yelling as loud as you can!

Loo

There's nothing worse than climbing down a slippery ladder in the teeming rain! And chemical loos used to smell awful. A very good modern edition is the 'Porta Potti 265'. This is sealed against bad smells and only needs emptying every few weeks. Put a cushion on top of it, and it becomes part of the furniture. For privacy it is just as well to make a tiny annexe with a partition wall and a simple door or curtain.

Furniture

The obvious table, shelves, old sofa, possibly a folding table – but it is a chore to have to keep clearing things away.

Sink units

Good lightweight small plastic sink units can be obtained from old VW caravanettes. If you want to DIY, buy a plastic washing-up bowl and plumb it by drilling out a plughole and fitting a drainaway unit. For the actual unit, hacksaw the right size hole in a piece of chipboard, and nail this onto a wooden frame. A flexible hose and a gutter tube to soak away into the ground will constitute the drainage system.

Another source of sink water can be an overhead gravity-feed water tank, filled by garden hosepipe or water off the roof. Another system is a caravan water tank with a foot-pedal pump.

Treehouse extras include an adequate supply of candles and matches; a long length of rope in case of emergencies. Insecticide; a wide range of drinks to suit every taste; tea bags, a bottle-opener and a corkscrew. The best spare beds are hammocks just so long as the visitors do not mind swaying amid the neighbouring branches, holding an umbrella over their heads!

Treehouse construction 'play kits' made from interlocking polypropylene components are obtainable from Early Learning Centre Shops. These versatile frame kits can fit up any tree. The 'Quadro' kit is priced at £130. All the components are weatherproof, strong and lightweight. The tubes and connectors are secured safely by a simple locking key. The Quadro kit includes 137 pieces and numerous side panels. It is probably rightly claimed that it helps develop children's agility and imagination. Another advantage is that, if they get bored with their treehouse, you can take it apart and rebuilt it into anything your child wants – a tunnel, a slide . . . For access you will probably have to buy another unit, or a giant climbing frame (£60), from which to construct a ladder. Or you could simply purchase a rope ladder at £5 – five wooden rungs and a rot-proof polypropylene rope.

It should be emphasized that the Quadro playhouse is basically a frame. For something more enclosed, Early Learning Centres offer a complete playhouse at £150. Moulded in sturdy polythene that will not chip, peel or splinter, it has two large windows with shutters that open and close and a Dutch-style roof providing access to the inside. The interior has a drop-leaf table providing plenty of room for pretend play. Even a play telephone with a clicking dial is included. It is easily assembled with bolt-together construction. ($45 \times 41 \times 48$ inches high.)

Naming the Treehouse

Proud treehouse owners will inevitably feel inclined to baptize their creation, if only as a good excuse for a party. The Swiss Family Robinson enjoyed a similar experience: 'The most difficult point was to name our present abode. At last we agreed on Falcon's Nest (in German Falken-hoist). This was received with acclamations, and I poured out for my young nestlings each a glass of sweet wine, to drink Prosperity to Falcon's Nest.'

Pooh Bear, for some reason – certainly not known to himself, occupies a hollow treehouse with the nameplate of a Mr Sanders inscribed above the door. In another part of the forest Christopher Robin dwells in a hollow tree with a green door, while Piglet resides in a very grand treehouse in the middle of a beech tree. Next to his house is a piece of broken board with 'Trespassers W' on it. Piglet claims it is his grandfather's name, W being short for Will, and Will short for William. Perhaps the grandest treehouse of all belongs to Owl:

> Owl lived at The Chestnuts, an old-world residence of great charm, which was grander than anybody else's, or seemed so to Bear, because it had both a knocker *and* a bell-pull. Underneath the knocker there was a notice which said:
> PLES RING IF AN RNSER IS REQIRD.

Garden Design

For most of the last hundred years and for most people, treehouses have been relegated to playhouses for adventurous children. Banished virtually to oblivion, no longer are they even considered part of garden design. As we have seen, this was not always so, and nor need it be nowadays. Any imaginative person, with a patch of back garden, a bit of DIY and some sort of tree (even poles and climbing creepers will suffice) can create a charming summerhouse effect a few feet up in the sky, and save space at the same time. Even better for those lucky enough to possess a blossoming cherry or almond tree. While if you happen to have a bit more land with an unusual feature such as a tree by a stream or a spinney, a charming and original away-from-it-all treehouse is a practical and pleasant prospect.

The intriguing feature of treehouses is the illusory effect once you are up in them. The treehouse may be only six feet above ground but once you have climbed up, you feel you are three times that height, as well as entering another element – the sky. What more ideal location for birdwatching? You could even add a pigeonloft. Squirrels are quick to befriend their new neighbour even if they do have the irritating habit of using the roof as a launch pad.

A Treehouse for You?

Since I started researching this book, I have been surprised by the amount of interest in treehouses shown by everyone. It is certainly an evocative topic. As a result, I have persuaded Ralph Curry, recently returned from opal-mining in Australia, to be prepared to go forth and create custom-made treehouses to suit.

We have spent a number of absorbing evenings in his treehouse or mine drawing up plans for a variety of models. There is the John Evelyn post-Renaissance design, with or without domed cupola, and the Plessis-Robinson French bower model. For the Neanderthal-minded there is the thatched Bradford Carpet, for the new Elizabethan the Pitchford Hall. And for those with spreading lime trees there is the Cobham Hall, interlacing branches model (patents applied for). If you have a hollow tree, you may be tempted to emulate Clifford Matthews' 'Snow White' house at Ventnor.

But on one thing be assured: if either your imagination or your practical skill grinds to a halt, there are now two treehouse specialists – one a qualified BF (Bachelor of Forestry). Smoke signals, pigeonpost, even voodoo drum messages are all acknowledged. Treehouses are on their way again – the new UP-market garden design! Ideal for *al fresco* bridge parties, getting rid of mother-in-law and spying on your neighbour's prize dahlias over the hedge. You might even go in for such extras as matching Tarzan and Jane outfits, or surprise the postman with a friendly jungle call as you swing down the rope to collect the morning mail.

Index

Abbot's Oak, 97
Acton Burnel, 49
'Adam' and 'Eve', 126–9
Aldworth, 101
Allouville-Bellefosse, 114–19
Anglesey, Marquess of, 60–2
Apicius, 32
Arno, River, 33
Arthur, King, 155
Arthur, Tom, 139
Asterix, 161
Augustine, St, 98, 118
Au Vieux Chêne, 109

Bangor University, 19
Barfreston, 101
Barham, 80
Barrie, J. M., 87, 104
Battersea Fun Fair, 126
Baxter, James K., 158, 159
Bayliss, Anthony, 105–7
Bayly, Sir Nicholas, 61
Belton House, 62–5
Bevin, John, 92
Blake, Charles Dupee, 155
Blount, 94
Blyton, Enid, 160, 161
Boiven, John, 50
Bol, Hans, 41
Boracay, 20
Bosch, Hieronymus, 15, 41, 42
Boscobel, 17, 93
Boyce, Jay, 87
Brabourne, 101
Bradford, Earl of, 27
Bradford Table Carpet, 27, 188
Brassey, T., 129

Brent-Dyer, Elinor M., 130
Brisley, Joyce Lankester, 161
Brohier, Nesta, 148–50
Brownlow, Sir John, 62
Brueghel, Pieter, 15, 41
Bryant, Arthur, 66, 93, 94
building tips, 169
  bridges, 40, 74, 75
  Chestnuts treehouse, 160
  choice of tree, 171–3
  Clifford Matthews's treehouse, 103
  Churchill's treehouse, 70
  Cobham Hall arbours, 42
  communications, 47, 183
  doors, 181
  Early-Learning Centre kits, 186
  extra equipment, 185
  floors, 181
  furniture, 185
  garden treehouses, 187
  heating, 181
  hunters' hides, 142
  John Evelyn's design, 45
  ladders, 45, 78, 179, 180
  lavatories, 185
  lighting, 182
  Milly-Molly-Mandy's treehouse, 161
  platforms, 167, 174, 175
  roofs, 176
  St Margaret's Bay treehouse, 22, 23
  sink units, 185
  Solomon Islands treehouse, 20
  spiral staircases, Pratolino, 37
  supports, 81, 174

building tips – *cont.*
  Swiss Family Robinson's construction, 182
  Tarzan's treehouse, 178
  walls, 180
  water systems, 183, 184
  windows, 180
  Wizard King's treehouse, 166
  wood butcher's art, 81–3, 145, 146
Burghley, 51
Burroughs, E. R., 147, 164, 177, 179

Calcutta Botanical Gardens, 151
Caligula, Emperor, 15, 18, 28, 32
Cameron, Dr, 95
Careless (Carlos), Colonel, 94
Castello, 33, 36, 37
Chandos Street, 125
Charles I, 42
Charles II, 17, 66, 68, 93–5
Chartwell, 68–70
Chelsea Pensioners, 95
Chevalier, Maurice, 111
Chilham, 84–7
Christ Church College, Oxford, 45
Christopher Robin, 161, 186
Churchill College Library, 69
Churchill, Sarah, 70
Churchill, Winston, 68–70
Church Stretton, 89–91
Clayton family, 169
Cluny's Cage, 95–7
Cobham Hall, 42, 44, 45, 188
Cock, Hieronymous, 41
Coleridge, S. T., 46, 47
Colonna, Francesco, 35
Colthurst, Caroline, 49, 55–60
Columbus, Christopher, 26
Conqueror's Oak, 97
Cook, Capt. James, 25
Corbett, Col. Jim, 139
Cornwallis-West, George, 70
Cowthorpe Oak, 99
Crane, Sidney, 148
Cressage Oak, 98, 118
Curry, Ralph, 80–4, 173, 187

Darley Churchyard, 101
Davies, W. H., 92
de Crescenzi, Piero, 36
Defoe, Daniel, 164
Dehra Dun, Uttar Pradesh, 150
della Bella, Stephano, 37
Dover Straits, 23
Downing, John and Leslie, 73–8
Dropmore, 94

Early-Learning Centre Shops, 186
Edward I, 97
Elizabeth I, 15, 18, 44, 51, 97
Elizabeth II, 15, 18, 138
Elizabeth, the Queen Mother, 55, 139
Ely, Bishop of, 123
Ely Place, 123
English Heritage, 97, 107
Ethelbert, King, 118
Evelyn, John, 45, 94, 101, 188

Fenni, 26
Festival of Britain, 126
Fitzherbert, Basil, 94
Forestry Commission, 103
Fortingal, 101
Francisci, Erasmus, 26

Gadsden, Sir Peter, 60
George V, 53, 55
George VI, 18, 55
Gibson, Major Charles, 15, 164–6
Glastonbury, 156
Gloucester, Duke of, 137, 151
Gloucester Tree, 151
Gosport, 87
Grant, Sir Charles, 55
Grant, Lady Sybil, 55, 56
Grant, Robin, 55, 56
Gray, Thomas, 101
Great Western Railway, 18
Grenville, Lady, 94
Greville, Hon. Louis, 68
Grey, Walter, the Archer, 120–2
Greystoke, Lord (John Clayton) and Lady Alice, 178
ap Griffith, Gwylym, 61
Guadalcanal, 20

Gueusquin, Joseph, 111

Hahgalla, 151
Hainhausen, 41
Hakshi, Major General, 150
Hanover, Elector of, 96
Happy Eater, Hogs Back, 106, 107
Hatton Garden, 125
Hatton, Sir Christopher, 123
Haverford, 47
Heale House, 66–8
Henry IV, 93
Henry VIII, 97
Hewagama, 148–50
Hillaby, John, 89, 91
Historic Buildings Council, 59
Holinshed, Raphael, 44
Holloway, Sarah, 150
Hollywood, 107
Honour Oak, 102
Hood, Robin, 15, 17, 97, 98
House in the Tree Pub, 120–2
House on the Hill, 73–8

John de Pitchford, 50
Johnson, Isaac, 132

Kent County Council, 19
Ket, 'King', 97
Kew Gardens, 125
Kingsland, 130

Lear, Edward, 161–3
Lennon, John, 18
Leonard Cheshire Foundation, 150
Liberty Oak, 101
Lichfield, Bishop of, 94
Licinius, Mucianus, 28
Liverpool, Earl of, 53
Lloyd Wright, Frank, 145
Lochiel, 95
Lochigarry, 95
Lycia, 28

MacMillan, H. F., 19, 148, 151
Macpherson, Ewen 'Cluny', 95
Major Oak, 47, 58, 97, 98
Mamhilad, 101

Mary, Queen Consort, 53, 55
Masai, 142
Mason, John Ltd., 57
Matthews, Clifford, 102–4, 188
Matthews, Hilton, 103
Meavy, 99
Medici, 33, 36, 37
Melbourne Hall, 130
Melville, Rodney, 57, 58
Menuhin, Sir Yehudi, 18
Meru tribesmen, 18
Middle Woodford, 66
Mills, G. K., 128
Milly-Molly-Mandy, 161
Milne, A. A., 15
Mitre Pub, 123–5
de Montaigne, Michel, 37
Monte Merello, 33
Morland, John, 155, 156
Morrison, Fynnes, 37, 51
Moulin Rouge, 109
Mountbatten, Earl, 149
Mount Elgon, 18
Mousley, T. & Sons, 57
Murray, Lord George, 95

National Library of Wales, 56
National Trust, 62, 64, 65, 104
Normandy, William of, 97
Notre Dame, 114–19

Order of the Sealed Knot, 95
Ordnance Survey, 49
Orinoco River, 26
Ottley, Sir Francis, 52
Ottley, Thomas, 50
Owen Glendower's Oak, 92, 93

Paget, Baron, 61
Paget, Lady Amelia, 60, 62
Papamanchua, 20
Papua, 18
Parambitulam, 150
Parkinson, John, 42, 44, 51
Parliament Oak, 97
Pendrill, William, 94
Percy, Sir Henry (Hotspur), 93
Philadelphia, 47
Philip, Prince, 138
Pino Santo, 114

Pitchford Hall, 47, 49–60, 188
Pitt, Henry, 99
Plas Newydd, 60–2, 70
Plaxton, Revd G., 94
Plessy Robinson Restaurant, 110, 188
Pliny the Elder, 28
Pooh Bear, 17, 161, 186
Pope, Alexander, 92
Potter, Beatrix, 155
Pratolino, 33, 37

Queen's Oak, 97

Raleigh, Sir Walter, 26, 27
Rasch, Lady Anne, 68
Reformation Oak, 97
Reggiani, Serge, 112
River Dart Country Park, 65, 66
Rolleston-on-Dove, 78–80
Rosebery, Earl of, 55
Rosemaund Oak, 47, 99, 100
Ross, John, 47
Rothschild, Hanna, 55
Royal Botanical Gardens, Peradeniya, 19, 151

St John's Wood church, 125
St Margaret's Bay, 22
Salisbury Hall, 70
Schaffhausen, 37
Scissors Tree, 132
Shakespeare, William, 113, 123, 164
Sheldrick, Capt. 'Ugly', 135, 136
Shercliff, Josephine, 78, 80
Shrewsbury and Atchum Borough Council, 57
Shropshire County Council Sites and Monuments Records, 50
Signoret, Simon, 112
Simpson, S. P. W. J., 65
Society for the Protection of Ancient Buildings, 49
Solomon Islands, 20
Stapleton, Mrs. Bettina, 80
Stevenson, R. L., 96, 97
Stoke Poges, 101
Straughan, R. P., 140
Stuart, Charles (Bonny Prince Charlie), 95–7
Stubbs, Joanna, 159
Stukeley, Dr, 94
Sumithraarachchi, Mr, 151
Swiss Family Robinson, 17, 164, 179, 181, 182, 186

Tally Ho Pub, 104
Tarzan (Lord Greystoke), 17, 147, 148, 164, 177, 178
Tennyson, Alfred Lord, 101
Thurston, John, 146, 147
Tien-Shih Chai Hua-Pao, 25
Tinitinas, 26
Tolkien, J. R. R., 158
Treetops, 18, 135–40, 179, 183
Tribolo, 33, 35
Tudur, Morfed, 61
Tuscany, 36

Vasari, 35
Victoria, Queen, 15, 47, 53
Villa Petrai, 37
Vrai Arbre de Robinson, 111, 112
Vriedenen de Vries, Hans, 41

Wales, Prince of, 74
Walker, Eric and Lady Betty Sherbrook, 135, 136, 179, 183
Wallace, Sir William, 99
Wallace's Oak, 99
Waterloo, 61
Weismuller, Johnny, 147
Wellington, Duke of, 61
Whistler, Rex, 61, 62
William I, 97
Willock, Henry and Sons, 58
Woburn, Abbot of, 97
Woodersons (shirt makers), 125
Wood Street, 125
Woolhope Naturalist Field Club, 99, 127
Worcester, Battle of, 17
Wordsworth, William, 125
Worlingham Common, 18, 92, 130, 132
Wyss, J. R., 164, 179

York, Duke of, 61